Library of Congress Control Number: 2011925142

ISBN 978-0-7624-3984-3

Running Press Book Publishers
2300 Chestnut Street
Philadelphia, PA 19103-4371

Visit us on the web!

www.runningpress.com

Editorial Manager: Roland Hall
Design: Lucy Coley/ James Pople
Layout: A+E
Picture Research: Ben White
Production: Claire Halligan

Printed in Dubai

EAGLES

TAKING IT TO THE LIMIT

BEN FONG-TORRES

RUNNING PRESS
PHILADELPHIA · LONDON

CONTENTS

INTRODUCTION

MY ENCOUNTERS WITH THE EAGLES

1978: This is weird. I am in what could pass as a baseball uniform. I have a bat in my

hand, and the P.A. announcer, who just happens to be Joe Smith, chairman of Elektra

Asylum Records, has just informed a sellout crowd of 5,000 that I am "now batting".

I step into the batter's box and peer out to the pitcher's mound. And there, ready to try to get me out, is Don Henley.

The Eagles' drummer and, often, its lead singer, is just one of several members of the band who are on the field. Don Felder, guitarist, is patrolling right field. Timothy Schmit, the hippie-haired bassist, is at third base. At first is Glenn Frey, the Eagles' co-captain, along with Henley. The always colorfully-dressed guitarist Joe Walsh was the starting catcher; now, in the ninth inning, he's on the bench.

The Eagles had shown up, this beautiful day in May 1978, for a softball game at Dedeaux Field, on the campus of the University of Southern California. Their opponent was *Rolling Stone* magazine, where I was an editor and writer.

The game was hyped as a grudge match. The Eagles, the story went, were offended by snipes in the magazine's "Random Notes" gossip column, which apparently delighted in reporting the band's losses in charity softball games. The Eagles got to wondering: could those effete, bespectacled, typewriter-pounding know-it-alls do any better?

What better way to find out than yet another charity game? Especially against the biggest pop-culture magazine in the land, which might – just might – result in some publicity for both sides.

The Eagles – a name Frey favored because it sounded like it could be the name of a street gang – were ready to rumble. Besides all the band members, they had members of their road crew in the line-up, along with Peter Cetera of Chicago in the outfield. Until he injured himself at a practice, Jimmy Buffett was slated to be another ringer.

Rolling Stone took "the Gonzos" as a team name. They might as well have called us the Stoners. That was how we played. Five errors? A final score of Eagles 15 Gonzos 8? Where have you gone, Hunter S. Thompson?

The crowd didn't care. We were on Eagles turf, in L.A. *Rolling Stone* was from San Francisco, home of the hated Giants. And, just the summer before, the magazine had moved to New York, where no one liked the Eagles – no New York rock critics, anyway.

So, here in Los Angeles, the Eagles were not only the home team; they had, among the 5,000 fans that had gathered for the game, a few celebrity rooters. One of them was Joni Mitchell, the subject of my first cover story for *Rolling Stone*, back in 1969. She told a reporter, "I'm here as an enemy of *Rolling Stone*."

Ouch. Also there to cheer on the Eagles (and, I'm sure, to boo me when I entered the game as a pinch-hitter) were Chevy Chase, Daryl Hall (*sans* Oates), Donald Fagen (one of my all-time favorite musicians), Karla Bonoff, and the once and future California governor, Jerry Brown, who was dating Linda Ronstadt, another of my cover-story subjects and a pivotal figure in the very formation of the Eagles.

Hey, no pressure! We were down about 15–5, here in the top of the ninth when I stepped in against Henley. We had nothing to lose, especially since we'd pretty much lost already.

Both of the Los Angeles newspapers covered the game. This was a big deal. In the *Herald Examiner*, Bobby Shriver wrote:

In the top of the ninth, the Gonzos stage a rally. Wenner pops off the bench, lights a fresh smoke, and begins making line-up changes. Writer Ben Fong-Torres goes into the game and the crowd applauds when he is introduced. "My God," Wenner says to his bench. "Ben gets a hand." He repeats in disbelief: "Ben gets a hand."

Wenner shouldn't have been surprised. Sure, the Eagles were said to harbor ill feelings for the magazine's New York-based critics, but I think a number of those Eagles rooters knew that I was also a fan of the band's; that I'd done articles on Crosby, Stills, Nash & Young, Linda Ronstadt, Bonnie Raitt and other L.A.-based artists. They didn't know, but, as a weekend DJ on KSAN, the free-form rock station in San Francisco, I played a lot of Eagles music – and Jackson Browne, Joni Mitchell and J.D. Souther, too. I wasn't one of *those* New Yorkers.

Raised on Top 40 radio, with its democratic rotation of all kinds of music, I became a fan of country and R&B as well as rock and pop. I enjoyed many of the artists who'd paved the way for the Eagles, from Elvis and the Everly Brothers to the Beatles, the Byrds and the Flying Burrito Brothers. I'd been a lifelong admirer of harmony groups, from the doo-wop of the Chords and the Belmonts to the close-harmony pop of the Four Freshmen and the Four Preps to the Motown sounds of the Temptations and the Pips behind Gladys Knight, and the stylings of Peter, Paul & Mary and the Limeliters, to the rock-era synchronicity of the Beach Boys, the Association, the Beau Brummels, Peter & Gordon, the Kinks, the Hollies and so many others. I was an appreciator of clever lyrics and close harmonies. The Eagles fit right into my mental music library.

Glaring at me from the pitcher's mound, Don Henley didn't care how many times I'd played "Life in the Fast Lane"

My Encounters With the Eagles

> *Eagles – a name Frey favored because it sounded like it could be the name of a street gang – were ready to rumble.*

ABOVE: The author, alongside Editorial Assistant Cynthia Bowman, prepares for a duel with the Eagles.

PREVIOUS PAGE: Peter Cetera, Glenn Frey and Timothy B. Schmit line up for the Eagles.

TOP: The *Rolling Stone* dugout: Dave Marsh, Jann Wenner, Ben Fong-Torres.

ABOVE: Howard Kohn, Rich Wiseman, Ben Fong-Torres.

> *They gave us a glimpse of their determination and will to win.*

or "New Kid in Town" on the radio. He just wanted to get me out.

I don't recall the sequence of Henley's pitches. Actually, if it weren't for the newspaper coverage, I'd have nothing at all. But I'm pretty sure I smacked several pitches into the stands, just foul, before grounding into a fielder's choice. So, I went oh-for-one, but we scored three runs to close the gap.

In the long run, *Rolling Stone* lost… and won. The Eagles, by winning, earned the right to write their own story, under the bylines of Frey and Henley, about how they vanquished the evil music press. If the Gonzos had won, Frey and Henley would have submitted to an interview, something they had refused to do for several years.

Same difference. We won. *We Are the Champions!*

But, of course, it was the Eagles who were victorious. It was fated. The game reminded us, and the rest of the press, of their power and popularity. Here, in the spring of 1978, they were still riding high on the triumphs of *Hotel California*. On the field, they gave us a glimpse of their determination and will to win. Sure, there was talk about bad craziness behind the scenes, but on the charts, on stage, and, now, on the softball diamond, they were undeniable.

In their six years of existence, they'd soared to the upper reaches of the pop charts again and again: "Take It Easy", "Witchy Woman", "Peaceful Easy Feeling", "Best of My Love", "One of These Nights", "Lyin' Eyes", "Take It To The Limit", "New Kid in Town", "Hotel California" and "Life in the Fast Lane."

And now they had beaten us, fair and square. With grudging admiration, we joined them in a post-game party at Dan Tana's, an in-crowd Italian restaurant steps away from the Troubadour. None of us, as far as I know, stooped so low as to pose for photos with the rock stars, but, for my KSAN show, I grabbed sound bites from Glenn and Joe and Chevy Chase. We ate and drank together, and others, perhaps, did more. In the end, there were no losers, except for us.

But, behind the scenes, the Eagles weren't having it all that easy. They were seesawing between a new album, that would be called *The Long Run*, and touring. Both in the studios (in Los Angeles and Coconut Grove, Florida) and on the road, trouble was brewing.

We, the useless wretches of the rock press, didn't know it but the Eagles were, in fact, nearing the end of their long run. Within two years, they would be torn asunder, an absolutely dysfunctional group of exhausted, embittered musicians. They slowly, quietly broke up. And when the media asked when they might get back together again, Don Henley famously said: "When Hell freezes over."

2005: I am facing Don Henley again. He is neither on a pitcher's mound nor on the stage. He is on a stationary bicycle. It is moments before the Eagles take the stage at the

LEFT: Glenn Frey savors the sweet taste of victory after the Eagles defeat *Rolling Stone* magazine.

Madison Square Garden this spring evening in New York. They had disbanded, officially, in 1982, reunited in 1994, and now appear to be working as hard as ever. Here in April of 2005, they are winding down their "Farewell I Tour," as it is slyly named. And, in a small room away from the dressing rooms and green rooms, Henley is pumping away on his bike. He will do this for a full 30 minutes, he says, "to get the blood pumping and get sweaty." Then he will do stretches, "because playing the drums is hard on the lower back. So this has become more of an athletic event than an artistic adventure at this juncture."

And the Garden, behind the scenes, feels more like business than show. As Henley put it: "Things are a lot calmer now… there's not all the drama and chaos there was in the Seventies… It's like a morgue backstage."

In the bowels of Madison Square Garden, where the concrete walls are decorated with more hockey players than rock stars (although there are framed shots of U2, Michael Jackson and Elvis, along with Sinatra, Pavorotti and George Burns), the other Eagles are in their own worlds, going through their own pre-show rituals.

Joe Walsh, who was already experienced when he was roped into the Eagles in late 1975, between their fourth and fifth studio albums (*One of These Nights* and *Hotel California*), was the wildest of wild men, an American version of Keith Moon. No more. We were talking about the Eagles' concerts in Melbourne, Australia and whether or not he'd sampled the nightlife there. "Not really," he said. "Having discovered sleep." He laughed. "I need to sleep to be able to do what I do. I work out and sleep."

Timothy B. Schmit, the bassist who sings the high notes on songs like "Take It To The Limit" and "I Can't Tell You Why", tells me that he does vocal exercises with a recording. "I was getting a strain in my voice, so I went to a vocal guy and he's teaching me to keep my voice by singing more correctly. I want to keep my voice as long as I can."

Just before show time, Timothy is in his dressing room, doing a meet-and-greet with employees of Netjets, who provide air transportation for the Eagles. It's so civil backstage that I have to ask him to compare now with then. I'd heard about the Eagles' backstage scene amounting to nothing less than sex, drugs and rock 'n' roll.

"Yeah," he replies. "Pretty much." He has a momentary flashback. "We were younger. We were traveling; it was newer to us; we didn't have big families with us; we weren't wiser."

I was seeing Timothy, Joe, Don and Glenn Frey for a piece for *TV Guide*. The hook was that NBC would be airing an Eagles special, filmed while they were on the Melbourne leg of the tour. A longer version would also be released globally on DVD.

It was my first real trip with the Eagles, after all these years. Sure, there was the softball game and the after party at Dan Tana's, but who remembers any of that? And there certainly was no interviewing going on before, during or after the game.

My Encounters With the Eagles

This was my first sit-down with the Eagles and I found a rock band in middle age and, all in all, dealing with it pretty well. Unlike so many pop and rock artists hitting their fifties, they weren't in denial.

"We can't do what we used to do," Joe Walsh said. In the good old days, he could destroy hotel rooms with the best of them. I mean, did even Keith Moon carry a chainsaw with him on tour?

"Used to be: we'd stay up all night and go to the next gig. Have parties with a billion people and we can't do that any more. I really can't do three shows in a row. We're trashed after three in a row."

Now, he does vocal warm-ups before a show. In the old days: "I drank vodka. *That* was my warm-up routine. Coat my stomach with some vodka. And then start drinking!"

When I saw them in New York, the Eagles were aged 56 to 58 and could well afford to retire. *Eagles – Their Greatest Hits 1971-1975* is one of the best-selling albums of all time, and their 2004 earnings were estimated to be $27.3m. Irving Azoff, their

manager of 30 years standing, boasted that they had "taken $1.5m out of the Garden."

They weren't in denial about their capitalistic instincts. "We get paid a lot of money," Frey said in his grand suite the day after the show. "But I feel we've earned it by virtue of how long we've survived. We didn't set out to be a band for all times. We set out to be a band for our times. And sometimes, if you're good enough to be a band for your time, you become a band for all time."

They had also become a band for all purposes, including corporate events. Almost all big-league performers do them, Azoff told me: Elton John, Billy Joel, Rod Stewart – even the Rolling Stones. "They get about a million a pop."

The Eagles, he said, had done only a few. "My rule of thumb is to double what you make on your biggest gig. If

these guys want you bad enough…" he said, not needing to complete the sentence.

I found myself in a state of wonderment at all this and to be seeing the Eagles and Azoff after all these years. Back in 1978, at that softball diamond in Los Angeles, Azoff had worn a jersey with customized lettering:

Is Jann Wenner Tragically Hip?

In 2005, the jersey had been answered. Wenner, at 60, was doing just fine. And so was Azoff, trailing along with his charges, just a few years behind.

Over dinner, just before we headed out to the Garden, Azoff told me something I'd never known. We had flashed

My Encounters With the Eagles

It was only one show, but the back-up band that evening consisted of Glenn Frey, Don Henley, Randy Meisner, and Bernie Leadon.

I made all my musical contacts, and found people who were sympathetic to the musical styles I wanted to explore."

Ronstadt, who came to Los Angeles from Tucson, Arizona, where she had been raised on a wide range of music, from her father's favored Mexican ballads to Frank Sinatra and Hank Williams, noted: "There'd been a long period of time where country music had not impacted on pop music or rock 'n' roll. There was pure country stuff… but people weren't mixing the two."

In Los Angeles, they began to. Said Al Perkins, a guitarist with Shiloh who would later join the Flying Burrito Brothers and work on Gram Parsons' solo albums: "I think people gravitated toward one another, particularly in country rock, because it was new and fun, this fusion of acoustic music, bluegrass, country, and rock being born."

Ronstadt did her share of gravitating. She had scored a hit with the Stone Poneys with "Different Drum", which was composed by Michael Nesmith, best known as a Monkee, but a talented singer and songwriter who helped pave the country-rock road. She had gone solo and made a couple of albums with mixed results. Now, early in 1971, she was heading out on tour again and needed a back-up band. She turned to her producer,

John Boylan, to find and hire the necessary musicians. As Glenn Frey would later recount: "They wanted to put together a super rock group to back up Linda… they started talking about members of the Burritos and Poco." Whoever they wanted, they didn't have to go far, given all the talent that was hanging out in the Troubadour bar.

They tapped Glenn Frey, a hotshot out of Detroit who was going nowhere slow in Los Angeles, to play guitar. He, in turn, would tell a Texan he'd met, either at a record-company office or the bar at the Troub, about the gig. That was Don Henley, a drummer and singer. Boylan also invited a couple of better-known musicians to join the ensemble, if only for a night or two. They were Randy Meisner, a bass player who, as well as Poco, had had a short stint with the Stone Canyon Band, and Bernie Leadon, a virtuoso country and bluegrass picker who'd been one of the Flying Burrito Brothers. He'd worked with Ronstadt before and was happy to join the other guys for an engagement at Disneyland.

It was only one show, but the back-up band that evening consisted of Glenn Frey, Don Henley, Randy Meisner, and Bernie Leadon.

Ladies and gentlemen: The Eagles!

PREVIOUS PAGE: The ten Grammy Award-winning Linda Ronsdadt, pictured here in 1968 while still a member of the Stone Poneys.

LEFT: Before the Eagles, Bernie Leadon played in The Flying Burrito Brothers, pictured here in 1969. Back row: Michael Clarke, Leadon, Pete Kleinow; Front row: Chris Hillman, Gram Parsons.

2
MEET THE EAGLES

The birth of the Eagles can be traced to any number of people, including Ronstadt, Boylan, Frey and Rich Bowden, a childhood buddy of Henley's who gave him his first gig as a drummer. But since it was Frey who made the first move at the Troubadour, telling Henley about an opening in Linda's back-up band, we begin with the piston from Detroit.

The youngest of the seven men who would become Eagles, Glenn Frey was born November 6, 1948. His father was a mechanic/machinist who helped to build automobile parts.

"I grew up running," he said. "My father was a machinist in a shop that built the machines that build car parts... I went to school with the sons and daughters of automobile factory workers – fathers who beat their wives and kids. The kids would then go to school and beat on me!" But, he said, "I had a pretty normal childhood. My parents weren't drinkers. I always had clothes. I always went to camp for a week in the summer. My parents didn't have enough money to buy me a car when I turned 16, but I had a great childhood."

At age five, his parents had him taking piano lessons. Although he got good enough to perform recitals, he became more interested in sports and rock 'n' roll. He was a natural athlete who wrestled and loved baseball, but as a kid discovering the opposite sex, he quickly learned about the potential powers of music – not classical tunes on a piano, but the stuff that got the girls all riled up.

In high school, Glenn came to be known as "the teen king" – or maybe he just called himself that. He was bright, had the gift of the gab, played some baseball and, now, began teaching himself how to play the guitar. In September 1964, on the eve of his 16th birthday, his life changed.

"My aunt got tickets to see the Beatles, and it was just an amazing experience," he said. He saw two half-hour shows at the Olympia Stadium in Detroit. "You barely heard the beginnings of each song, and it was just these waves of people screaming. This girl in the chair in front of me fell into my arms. She was screaming, 'Paul! Paul!' I thought, 'Wow! Man! This is really cool!'"

By the time Glenn graduated from high school in 1966, he was playing with bands ranging from the Subterraneans (originally called the Hideouts) and the Heavy Metal Kids to a folk-rock group, the Four Of Us, and the Mushrooms, who drew a following at a teen club. The Mushrooms cut a single, and, with Glenn on lead vocals and guitar, performed on a television dance show, Robin Seymour's *Swingin' Time*, starring the local Top 40 DJ.

Glenn had no interest in going away to college, as his mother Nellie wanted him to do. He agreed to attend a nearby community college. Glenn figured that would allow him to continue to gig around Detroit but Nellie went to her son's manager, Punch Andrews (who also managed local rocker Bob Seger). As she told Charles M. Young of *Rolling Stone*, "I asked him not to give Glenn any bookings unless he got good grades and stopped smoking marijuana." Andrews, apparently, couldn't make any such promise – especially after Frey met Seger, who'd scored several regional hits. "Seger was cool," said Frey. "I was never in his band but he liked me and let me come to some sessions when he was recording. He let me play maracas and, on one song, he let me play acoustic guitar. I also got to sing back-up vocals on 'Ramblin' Gamblin' Man', which was his first big hit."

While supposedly going to the community college, Frey continued to play with bands, once backing up Bo Diddley, and learned what was happening in California, north and south. An avid radio listener, he heard the music of the Byrds and Buffalo Springfield out of L.A., and when the Grateful Dead hit town to play the Grande Ballroom, Glenn was there. "I read about free love and free dope in California and said, 'That's the place for me.'" California, he said, struck him as "the archetype of the most beautiful place in the world".

LEFT: Bob Seger, circa 1969. He met Glenn Frey in Detroit in the 1960s, and he co-wrote "Heartache Tonight" from 1979's *The Long Run*.

RIGHT: The Grateful Dead were another influence on Glenn Frey. This photograph is from the *San Francisco Chronicle*, circa 1970.

In the summer of 1968, aged 19, Glenn told his parents he was leaving school and heading west to pursue a career in music. The way Nellie Frey heard it, "Glenn finally just told us to kiss off and packed up for California. 'Good luck,' I said. 'I can't give you anything now but love.'"

"My parents told me that if I was going to California, they weren't going to give me a goddamn dime," said Frey. Nellie, who by now was raising Glenn and his younger brother alone, the father having left the house, sent him a few dollars now and again. But Frey could take care of himself. He steered his pick-up to Los Angeles, to his girlfriend, and to where he figured the action was.

Don Henley was already there. Born a little over a year before Glenn, on July 22, 1947, he and Glenn had many differences, long before they ever met, but they traveled parallel paths. Born in the tiny town of Gilmer, Texas, and raised in the slightly less tiny farming town of Linden, Don was as serious and sensitive as Glenn was playful and rowdy.

While Glenn's father's work involved helping to manufacture automobile parts, Don's father operated a store in nearby Dangerfield that sold auto parts. Like Glenn, Don caught rock 'n' roll fever early on. He picked up country and blues music on the radio, sometimes pulling in bluegrass sounds from WNOE in New Orleans late at night, and caught onto R&B and early rock 'n' roll. Like millions of others, he became a big Elvis fan. And, like Glenn Frey, he was mesmerized by the Beatles, who served as a tonic for him.

Henley wasn't much interested in school and he was too small, he said, to be any good at sports. "One of the only things that kept me going was music, especially the Beatles," he told Robert Hilburn in 1982. "I would go in and listen to the Beatles records every morning just to get me through the day. I kept waiting until the day I could get out of school and out of town – on to some place where I would fit in better."

As a child, Don played the piano and then the trumpet and finally drums, which his mother, Hughlene, bought for him when he was 15, partly as a reward for Don's blowing up the family's primitive laundry cauldron with a cherry bomb, thus necessitating the purchase of a modern washing machine.

He played in a band started by a childhood buddy, Richard Bowden, called the Four Speeds, which was patterned after the guitar-driven Ventures and played only instrumentals. When it was decided that they needed to add vocals, no one volunteered. They picked the singer by drawing lots, and Don got the gig. The Speeds, later renamed Felicity, kept Don busy through high school, playing the American Legion Hall and the Lions Club in Linden. Their repertoire included covers of R&B hits. Straining to hit the high notes, Don developed a rasp that would become a trademark of his singing voice.

Don thought he'd found his career. But his parents wanted him to go to college, and so he did. His father, he once said, "was so intent on me having it better than he had had it that he saved 25 cents a day from the time I was born for my college education."

He went to Stephen F. Austin and North Texas State, tallying up the four years his parents wanted, but he never got a degree, as classrooms gave way to nightclubs and concert halls. But he did retain one indelible lesson.

"I had one English teacher who really turned my head around. He was way out of place in this little college. This bohemian, the first one I'd ever seen. He'd come to class in these outrageous clothes and lecture cross-legged on top of his desk. One day, he told me: 'Your parents are asking me what your future career plans are. I know there's a lot of pressure on

LEFT: Don Henley. Although usually the drummer with the Eagles, he also frequently plays guitar and sings.

RIGHT: Glenn Frey. In partnership with Henley, Frey has written many huge-selling hit songs despite the pair's ten-year break in the 1980s.

you to decide.' Then he said something I never forgot. 'Frankly, if it takes you your whole fucking life to find out what it is you want to do, you should take it. It's the journey that counts, not the end of it. That's when it's over.'"

Coming from Linden, population 2,000, said Don, "All you can do is dream." His dreams were mostly musical, and, too often, off-key. Felicity cut a local single that went nowhere. "We went through a number of small-time managers and played a lot of frat houses," Don remembered. Felicity became Shiloh, a country and bluegrass ensemble, after Al Perkins joined the band. Henley went to a Byrds concert in Shreveport in 1968 and saw the opening act, the Dillards. Shiloh combined country tunes with a hippie look and attitude. "We were long-hair pioneers," he said. "I was the first guy in town to smoke grass and to have my hair touch my ears."

Appearance does count, and it was while Don and a fellow Shiloh were in a boutique that they ran into Kenny Rogers, lead singer of the First Edition. They had scored the countrified Top 40 hit, "Just Dropped In (To See What Condition My Condition Was In)" in March 1968. It was spring 1969 and, as Henley recalled, "He was on tour with the First Edition. He had begun to look for groups to produce, so he checked us out, and

evidently formed the opinion that we had some potential. Of course, being fellow Texans didn't hurt: we had a regional and cultural connection."

They kept in touch, and, about a year later, Rogers summoned them to California to do some recording. Rogers was connected with the owner of a small label called Amos, and wanted to help them cut a demo – perhaps, even, a single.

Henley's dreams, which had often involved California, were on the verge of coming true. "I used to sit and watch the sun sink in the west and would say, 'Boy, the sun's going down in California. Some day I'm going to be there.'" The Golden State, he said, "was the dream of success…. the imagery, the music of the Beach Boys and the Byrds. It was the magazines I would read and the stuff I saw on television… California was always the promised land."

It's ironic that while Henley and Frey would emerge, a few years later, as the leaders of the Eagles, dominating the songwriting, the producing of the records and even the staging of their concerts, the two other original members were, in the beginning, more established musicians than either of them.

They, too, had been enlisted by Linda Ronstadt's producer, John Boylan, and included Henley's buddy Rich Bowden. Boylan also kept tabs on two players with pedigrees that made

them less likely candidates for backing up an up-and-coming singer like Ronstadt. Both Bernie Leadon and Randy Meisner were seasoned musicians from their times in such bands as the Flying Burrito Brothers and Poco. Both were well versed in the country part of country rock. But in the music business, work is work, and Leadon and Meisner were willing laborers.

Bernie Leadon is a native of Minneapolis, Minnesota, where he was born four days before Don Henley, on July 19, 1947. He and his siblings were the children of an aerospace engineer who moved several times – first to San Diego, California, when Bernie. He sang in his family's church choir and fell in love with music. By age 13, he was playing both the guitar and banjo, and later added bass guitar and mandolin. In late 1963 he was working professionally, picking banjo with the Scottsville Squirrel Barkers, who had future Byrd Chris Hillman on mandolin. The band had recorded an album, *Bluegrass Favorites*, before Bernie joined, and Leadon left the group the following year when he moved to Gainesville, Florida.

Then came 1964, the year of the Beatles' landing in America, putting an end to a folk-music run on the Top 40 charts. The way Bernie heard it, "The American folk era was mimicked in England by skiffle. That was followed by the rock

music of the British Invasion, which was British working-class kids echoing black American music. When that happened, those of us who could play and were younger just went, 'Wow!' I could already play, so we all ended up in bands, grew our hair out, got Beatles boots, Vox amps, and were off."

Still, he maintained his love of folk, country and bluegrass music, and split his time between the old and the new. He also spent time with a local guitarist he sought out on his arrival in town, reputed to be one of the best young players in Gainesville; Don Felder. Don taught Bernie to play electric guitar while Bernie got Don acclimated on acoustic. They later formed a rock band, the Maundy Quintet, which styled itself after bands of the British Invasion, and made money playing proms and fraternity parties.

Despite getting regular work, Leadon got itchy. "There's nothing here musically, man," he groused to Felder. "New York or California's where it's at, and I'm never gonna live in New York… One of these days I'm gonna blow, and just go back to California and make some real music."

Bernie, Felder said, also had problems with his parents, whose brood of kids grew to number ten. "Like my parents, they were often nagging him about what he was going to do with his life,

LEFT: An early-Eagles era Randy Meisner photographed in
Topanga Canyon, CA circa 1973.

37

and wanted him to pursue an academic career," Felder recalled
in his autobiography. "Bernie was upset that they weren't more
supportive."

Leadon left Gainesville in the middle of 1967, heading for
L.A. He had received an offer to join a group that had a deal
with a major record label.

In the three years he'd been gone from the West Coast, a lot
had changed. Several folk-musician friends he'd had in San Diego
had moved north to Los Angeles. One day, shopping for records,
he found an album by the Byrds with a familiar face on the cover –
Chris Hillman. He would soon reconnect with Hillman and such
like-minded pickers and singers as Clarence White, a folk guitarist
from Maine who would, like Hillman, wind up with the Byrds.

Another friend from San Diego was the guy who lured him
to Los Angeles. Larry Murray had formed a folk-rock group
called Hearts And Flowers, and had not forgotten about
Leadon's abilities with various instruments and musical genres,
as well as harmony vocal skills, learned in church and honed by
way of bluegrass music. Leadon initially replaced Rick Cunha in
the band.

"When he was 15 years old, he could play circles around
everybody," Murray recalled. "Bernie was exactly what we
needed. He was a great player… We needed more musical
dynamics, and Bernie added that."

Hearts And Flowers, with Leadon on guitar and banjo,
played various folk clubs around Los Angeles, often serving
as an opening act for star attractions. One of their regular
hangouts was the Troubadour. Bernie recalled: "We opened
there for people like Gordon Lightfoot, Arlo Guthrie, Judy
Collins. We played a lot."

During Leadon's nine months with the group, he performed
on an album, *Of Old Horses, Kids and Forgotten Women*. Through
Chris Hillman, he also met bluegrass banjo player Doug Dillard,
"always one of my idols", and began jamming with him. When
Dillard connected with ex-Byrd Gene Clark and scored a deal
with A&M Records, Leadon played bass and guitar on the
sessions for two excellent albums, *The Fantastic Expedition of
Dillard and Clark* (for which he also co-wrote half-a-dozen songs)
and *Through the Morning, Through the Night*.

When the Dillard And Clark expedition went wayward,
Leadon made himself available to others, including Linda
Ronstadt and John Boylan. He was part of the Corvettes, her
backup band when she toured her first solo album, *Hand Sown…
Home Grown*, in 1969. That fall, Hillman, who had left the
Byrds, recruited him to join him in the Flying Burrito Brothers,
alongside Clarence White and Gram Parsons. He pitched in
on two albums, playing lead guitar, but by the time he joined,
that incarnation of the Burritos were on the decline, with the
mercurial Parsons' attentions having drifted. "We had a working
group," he told me. "But – bad news for us – for three months,
Gram was over at Keith Richards' house all the goddamn time
and wouldn't show up for rehearsals. He just wanted to be with
Keith. The music, the chicks, the drugs."

Bernie quit and gravitated back to some of the Troubadour
crowd, including, once again, Ronstadt and Boylan. He was ripe
for the picking.

Meantime, Randy Meisner, like Leadon, had built a short but
impressive resume with Poco and the Stone Canyon Band. So
how was it that he was available for pick-up, back-up work?

Randy was the oldest and shyest of the Eagles. He was born
on a farm in Scottsbluff, Nebraska, on March 8, 1946. When
he was ten, he saw Elvis Presley on television, and suddenly the
farmer's boy visualized himself as a guitar-toting rock 'n' roll
star, making girls scream. It wasn't that far-fetched a notion: his
family was musical, and when he was nine, he was singing in
public, making his debut at a PTA meeting with "Honeycomb",
the 1957 hit by Jimmie Rodgers. His parents gave him a guitar,
and he could sing the songs of Elvis and Conway Twitty.

By 14, Randy was in a band, the Thunderbirds, playing Top
40 music. Soon, he found himself enjoying playing the bass
guitar while singing, naturally, at the other end of the scale,
with a high tenor voice.

At 15, while in high school, he was lead singer and bassist in
another band, the Dynamics, who paid (or whose parents paid)
to make a record. "The Dynamics started out as a Top 40 band
but mutated into a R&B band, which allowed me to do my
James Brown thing," he said. "When the Beatles came out, we
went totally the other way and started doing stuff by the Dave
Clark Five and all the English groups."

Randy was moving fast. In fact, by 16, he had fallen in love,
married, and had a baby boy. Throughout his early musical
career, he seesawed between gigs and home in Nebraska.

In 1965, the 17-year-old Randy and the (re-christened) Drivin' Dynamics went to Denver for a bands competition. They didn't win, but he met a competing band, the Soul Survivors, who had an opening for a bassist. He bade farewell to the Dynamics and told his wife, Jennifer, that he was going to Los Angeles with the Survivors. They did not survive the much tougher competition they found in Hollywood, and made a few changes, including adopting a new name: The Poor.

The Poor really were, said Randy. "There was one guy and his wife and four others living in a one-bedroom apartment. We slept on the floor."

The band got to make a recording, and they got a couple of bookings at the Whisky A Go Go. "But we were like the ones at the bottom of the totem pole," said Meisner. "We never really got anywhere." He did what he had to do to make money, including selling his car. One of his day jobs had him peddling newspapers along Sunset Strip. He also sold some of his stash of marijuana now and again to pay for his room at the funky motel, the Tropicana.

From his times at the Whisky, Randy met members of Buffalo Springfield. When that band broke up, two members, Richie Furay and Jim Messina, plotted out a new band and invited Randy to audition. He won out over, among others, a young bassist and singer, Timothy Schmit, and became part of Pogo.

Despite a splashy debut at the Troubadour and a string of fine recordings and well-attended concerts, Pogo – who by then were Poco – never attained the heights they expected. Within a year, Randy left, just as their debut album was being completed.

"There were various reasons for my leaving, but I finally quit over the final mix of the album," he said. "I wanted to be present to make my suggestions, but Richie and Jim said they were going to do it and that we'd have to wait and listen to it later." Meisner, who wanted a stronger bass and drum sound than he was hearing, responded by quitting. "I thought that if we were a group we should all have a hand in it," he said. In retrospect, he admitted, he acted too hastily. And the final album sounded good.

Richie Furay was conciliatory about Meisner in his 2006 book, *Pickin' Up the Pieces*. He noted that the mix-down sessions rightfully were placed in the hands of Messina, who had engineering and production experience, and that, with union regulations imposing limitations on what the musicians could do in the studio, they wanted as few interruptions as possible. "Maybe Randy caught us at a moment when we weren't as patient or understanding as we should have been," Furay reflected. "But it still seems strange that an incident as seemingly minor as this would have caused him to leave the band… He was a bit aloof compared to the rest of us and didn't fit into the Pogo family as well as we would have liked. If he felt the same way, he might have been looking for a way out."

Whatever the reason for his departure, it wouldn't be the last time Meisner would be in a band in which promises of equality – all for one; one for all – would be broken.

While Tim Schmit replaced him in Pogo/Poco, Meisner had by then gained the attention of other musicians around Los Angeles. One was Rick Nelson, the former teen idol. Nelson, whose first records mixed rockabilly and R&B, had seen Poco at the Troubadour and been inspired to go the country-rock route himself. Meisner recalls spotting Nelson in the audience: "It was like a big thrill. Rick Nelson's out there! Let's make sure we do a good job."

Nelson's producer was John Boylan, a New Yorker with a hip portfolio (he roomed with Chevy Chase, dated the actress Blythe Danner, and played music with Donald Fagen and Walter Becker, who would become the nucleus of Steely Dan). When Nelson expressed interest in forming a back-up band, Boylan called Meisner first, and he, in turn, called on a couple of his bandmates from The Poor.

Along with Tom Brumley, who'd played with Buck Owens, they became the Stone Canyon Band, and after playing a week at the Troubadour started recording. They cut an album, *Rick Nelson In Concert: The Troubadour, 1969* and had a modest hit with a version of Bob Dylan's "She Belongs to Me" in 1970.

Meisner was soon discontented, feeling like he was "getting nowhere, just backing someone up."

"I didn't feel I was getting a chance to express myself," he said. "It wasn't anyone's fault because it obviously had to be Rick Nelson and his group rather than just being a group with all the members having equal status." There it was – that equality thing again.

Meisner was frustrated, and so was his wife Jennifer, who asked him to return to Nebraska. He did. As a kid, he'd won blue ribbons for raising sheep. Now, he was back on the farm,

OVERLEAF: The Byrds, already a successful band by the time Frey arrived in LA.   RIGHT: Teen idol Ricky Nelson, photographed in 1968.

working for John Deere, the tractor company. But he couldn't resist music, played occasional gigs at night, and was soon drawn back to Los Angeles again. Once he showed up at the Troubadour bar, it was a matter of time before someone grabbed the talented bassist and singer for another band.

When they arrived in town, Glenn Frey and Don Henley were relative latecomers to the Troubadour and Los Angeles scenes. Members of the Byrds, Buffalo Springfield and other major bands had already moved on to other ensembles and adventures.

They were just beginning theirs. Both got right into the L.A. scene; both made fortuitous connections. Frey recalls: "The first day I got to L.A., I saw David Crosby sitting on the steps of the Country Store in Laurel Canyon, wearing the same hat and green leather bat cape he had on for *Turn! Turn! Turn!* To me, that was an omen. I immediately met J.D. Souther, who was going with my girlfriend's sister, and we really hit it off." So much so that he and the Texas native formed Longbranch Pennywhistle, who signed a deal with Amos Records – the label that was also working with Henley's band Shiloh.

Jimmy Bowen, a former rockabilly artist (and a 1957 one-hit wonder with "I'm Stickin' With You") who had turned producer and record executive, had founded Amos. Frey and Souther had signed a publishing and recording deal with Tom Thacker, a friend of Bowen's, but when Bowen heard a demo of their music – "squarely in that acoustic folk country groove… fresh and upbeat, with just enough country to make me think back to the early Everlys" – he made a deal with Thacker and got Longbranch Pennywhistle onto Amos.

Frey and Souther – a native of Amarillo, Texas, and a handsome young man with dual gifts for writing songs and attracting women – would break up with their girlfriends. The two moved in together, into a low-rent apartment building in Echo Park, along with a younger singer-songwriter, Jackson Browne. When Browne found even cheaper digs in a downstairs apartment, he moved out. Frey recalled: "The three of us were all living there, listening to records or to Jackson. I'd just lay in bed and hear him practice downstairs. The piano was right below my bed. Those were great times."

On occasions they would write together, and the results included "Take It Easy," composed by Browne and Frey. But neither Longbranch Pennywhistle's records nor their label

RIGHT: J.D. Souther, who was in Longbranch Pennywhistle with Glenn Frey.

was making it, and Bowen soon folded his operation. In his memoirs, Bowen claims that he released the guys from their contract but Frey has contended for years that he and Souther were told that they couldn't make any more records, and visited Amos' office daily to ask for a release from their deal. "And they'd say 'No', so we'd go down to the Troubadour bar and get drunk."

"The bar", Frey said, was "full of tragic fucking characters: has-beens and hopefuls. Sure, it's brought a lot of music to people, but it's also infested with spiritual parasites who will rob you of your precious artistic energy. I was always worried about going down there because I thought people would think I had nothing better to do. Which was true."

But something was in the works. One evening, when Frey was having dinner with Souther and Linda Ronstadt at Nucleus Nuance, a restaurant in West Hollywood, J.D. told Frey that Linda needed a back-up band on tour, and suggested that he sign up.

When Boylan made the official offer, Frey had no hesitation. "The $200 per week with Linda was more than I'd seen in about three years in California. I got so excited because I'd never been on the road before, except riding a truck from Detroit to L.A."

He immediately thought about Don Henley.

Once in a while, both at the offices of Amos Records and at the Troub, Frey would run into Henley. But they never spoke. Henley had his own concerns. He and Shiloh had come out to California, at Kenny Rogers' invitation, to cut some sides. They'd made two trips, in early and mid-1970 to cut a single (which bombed), and an album (ditto).

Like Frey, Henley arrived into town and dove into the scene, visiting that hangout, as Frey put it, of "has-beens and hopefuls." He saw stars, including Neil Young of Buffalo Springfield, Graham Nash of Crosby, Stills and Nash, and Linda Ronstadt. "She was standing there in a little Daisy Mae dress, barefoot and scratchin' her ass. I thought, 'I've made it! I'm in heaven!'"

But after the Shiloh album followed their single into oblivion, Henley was back down to earth.

"I really didn't know anybody," he said. "I just hung around the Troubadour by myself. It was kind of pathetic, really. But

LEFT: Kenny Rogers (second from left) and the First Edition in 1969.

OVERLEAF: Ready to rock: Leadon, Henley, Meisner and Frey.

one night Glenn Frey invited me over to his table and bought me a beer. He said, 'What's going on?' I said, 'My group's not doing anything. Things are a drag.' And Glenn said, 'My partner and I are breaking up, too. And there's this guy named David Geffen' – who I didn't know from Adam – 'and there may be a deal in the works if a band could be put together.'"

"I said, 'That's nice.' And he said, 'In the meantime, do you want to go on the road with Linda Ronstadt and make 200 bucks a week?' I said, 'Sure, fine, I'd love it!' I'd never really been on the road before. So Glenn and I became good friends and we started plotting and planning."

Frey and Henley initially played with other musicians that Boylan had hired. But Boylan also called on the best talent available, from established bands, if possible. And so it was that for a gig on July 12, 1971, at Disneyland in Anaheim that the two played with Leadon and Meisner.

The future Eagles played together behind Ronstadt only for one concert, but they reconvened to play on her third solo album, called *Linda Ronstadt*. By then, they knew they'd go off on their own, and Linda knew it, too.

"I knew Glenn was a temporary thing," she told me. "I knew he was going to be a star the minute I met him; he was such a hot shot. I loved him." But she'd seen a lot of back-up musicians come, play, and go. "When Glenn and Don met, they wanted to form a band right away."

As in the first night they were on tour with her. "The first stop," Frey remembered, "was the Cellar Door in Washington, D.C. After that first gig, Henley and I decided we'd start our own band."

Henley gives Ronstadt and Boylan credit for helping to start the Eagles. "John and Linda gave us their blessing," he said. "I really respect Linda Ronstadt. She's got a good heart. She's never been selfish enough to hold anybody back."

Another crucial early booster was J.D. Souther, who had dated Ronstadt and who had hipped Frey to the fact that she was looking for back-up players. Souther had already written some songs that would help launch the Eagles, and, for a time, he was considered as a member. It was not to be, and, from Souther's point of view, the band was perfect as a quartet. As soon as he heard them play together, he said, he knew. "It was just so damn obvious. So gorgeous, in-your-face obvious." The band was "a combination that worked beautifully", he said. "Someone from East Texas, a guy from Detroit, another from the Central Plains, and one from Florida. There was nothing Southern California about that band. They were an all-American rock 'n' roll outfit."

3

THE EAGLES TAKE OFF

Like a crack Detroit automaker, Glenn Frey had specific designs for his band. He had models, including the country-rock pioneers, the Flying Burrito Brothers and Poco. "We had it all planned," he said. "We'd watched bands like Poco and the Burrito Brothers lose their initial momentum. We were determined not to make the same mistakes. This was gonna be our best shot. Everybody had to look good, sing good, play good and write good. We wanted it all. Peer respect. AM and FM success. No. 1 singles and albums. Great music and a lot of money!"

They began by deciding, for a couple of different reasons, on a band name: Eagles. Not The Eagles; just Eagles. That idea, of course, didn't last, and the definite article was soon introduced.

For Frey, the name evoked a teen street gang. "Everybody wanted a name that was just tough," said Leadon. "'Hey, we're the fuckin' Eagles, man!' There was definitely a *West Side Story* aspect to it … 'We're the fuckin' Jets,' you know."

For Leadon, it was fuckin' spiritual as well. "We were reading books about the Hopis, and in the Hopi mythology the eagle is the most sacred animal, with the most spiritual meaning. The eagle flies closest to the sun and will carry our message to the father; it symbolizes all highest spirituality and morals… I would hope that the music would soar that high."

Also, it's been said, the guys didn't mind that "Eagles" sounded vaguely like "Beatles".

The not-quite-yet Fab Four had songs stockpiled from as far back as Frey and Souther's days living above Jackson Browne, and they worked up some new numbers then rehearsed for two weeks and made their pitch to David Geffen, who had begun his own record label, Asylum, with Joni Mitchell and Jackson Browne in the fold.

"So we got this rehearsal hall in the valley for a dollar an hour and rehearsed for two weeks solid," said Leadon. Geffen, he said, heard the band and made an offer.

Actually, Geffen was already sold. A wily agent-turned-manager-turned-record-label-head, he'd managed Laura Nyro and Browne, and had partnered with Elliot Roberts, manager of Joni Mitchell, Neil Young, and Crosby, Stills & Nash, in a powerhouse management company, Geffen-Roberts.

When I interviewed David Crosby for *Rolling Stone* in 1970, he minced no words in expressing his rather twisted appreciation of the two men. "Elliot Roberts is a good dude," he said. "He is not a fair weather friend… However, he is, in his managerial capacity, capable of lying straight-faced to anyone, anytime… And if he doesn't rob you blind, he'll send Dave Geffen over; he'll take your whole company. And sell it while you're out to lunch."

But Geffen was not simply a robber baron. He had an ear for talent. For starters, he had heard and signed up Nyro and Browne. And, he said, "Right after I signed Jackson, he talked

The Eagles Take Off

me into signing Glenn, which I did as a favor to him." When talk began about Frey, Henley, and company putting a band together, Geffen took care of some old business, buying out Longbranch Pennywhistle's and Shiloh's contracts from their labels.

Having worked with Crosby, Stills & Nash, Geffen knew winning combinations when he heard them. "Someone else wanted to add John David," he recalled, "but I didn't want to mess with what was working, and anyway, the thing I had liked most about John was his songs rather than his performing abilities. Glenn, I knew, was a born band creature."

Leadon recalled Geffen telling the band, "I won't give you any front money, but what I will do is give you advances; I'll support you until you get a hit record, as much money as it takes, but we'll give you a stringent accountant and it's gonna be tight, you know." It was a persuasive argument: "We went for that," said Leadon.

(Actually, said Henley, "He gave us something like two hundred bucks a week to live on while we rehearsed." They had not traveled far from their days backing up Linda Ronstadt.)

Geffen told the band that they needed some more work, and he found it for them in Aspen, Colorado, a nice distance from Hollywood. There, they got a month-long run at the Gallery Club. The idea was that the Eagles would try out their repertoire, such as it was. In the beginning, it was mostly R&B tunes Frey knew, and one or two new songs written by friends of the Eagles.

Meisner recalled: "We weren't really a cohesive group yet, although we did have that special sound. Still, it more was like an extended four-guy jam. We had a couple of songs that we did every night. 'Witchy Woman' was one of the first, and we did 'Take It Easy', a Jackson Browne song, more R&B, because that's the way Glenn played it… and a couple of Sonny Boy Williamson tunes. And a lot of Chuck Berry. Glenn loved to play Chuck Berry. We'd do four, sometimes five sets every night, and there were times when no one was in the house except maybe a bartender and a waitress or two, and a couple of hungry chicks. It was wild, kind of like what I imagine the Beatles went through in Germany."

Aspen wasn't all that much fun but Frey and Henley took it in their stride. They knew what they needed to do. Their models were some of the emerging stars back in Hollywood. As Frey put it: "Being around Geffen, and in close proximity to Jackson Browne, Joni Mitchell and Crosby, Stills & Nash, this unspoken thing was created between Henley and me, which said, 'If we want to be up here with the big boys, we'd better get our game together and write some fucking good songs!'" One way to do that was to distance themselves from those models, and from the Troubadour scene.

In Aspen, the audience included, one evening, a prominent record producer who'd been sent there by Geffen.

Glyn Johns had previously worked with the Rolling Stones and Led Zeppelin. Most recently, he'd produced the Faces' album, *A Nod's as Good as a Wink… To a Blind Horse*. Johns thought he'd be seeing and hearing a rock band when he arrived at the Gallery and heard the Eagles – who were calling themselves Teen King and the Emergencies for this run – and their mix of rock, R&B and country-rock. Whatever they were playing, he thought, it wasn't very good.

"They were playing Chuck Berry, badly," he said. "You had Bernie Leadon on one side, a great country player, and Glenn Frey on the other, a good rock 'n' roll guitarist, and they were pulling the rhythm section in two." He told Geffen that he wasn't interested in having the Teen King band follow the Stones and Led Zep in his discography.

But, Geffen being Geffen, he didn't give up, and persuaded the producer to see them again.

This time, Johns showed up early enough to catch a rehearsal. There, he spotted potential. "Bernie and Frey picked up acoustic guitars and played a song Randy had written – just two acoustics and four of them singing." And that, Johns said, was that: he was in.

Johns wanted to do his recording, as he always did, in London, at Olympic Studios. And so, in February 1972, the Eagles flew overseas – no doubt for the first time, at least for Henley and Frey – to make their first album.

From their time in Aspen, and from their inventory, the band had plenty with songs. They included "Take It Easy," the

---

CHAPTER OPENER: Dave Geffen in Los Angeles, California in 1973. He was instrumental in making the Eagles the successful act they became.

PREVIOUS PAGE LEFT: Jackson Browne played with the Eagles on a semi regular basis.

PREVIOUS PAGE RIGHT: David Crosby.

RIGHT: Glyn Johns was responsible for producing many all-time great albums, including *Eagles* and *Desperado* for the Eagles.

The Eagles Take Off

PREVIOUS PAGES: Meisner, Henley, Frey and
Leadon performing for Dutch TV in 1973.

BELOW and RIGHT: In the desert for the photo
shoot for the first album, *Eagles*. The group went into

the Joshua Tree National Park to 'take peyote and
commune with nature'.

Jackson Browne song that seemed to epitomize the California dream – at least the part of it that involved a footloose, laissez-faire lifestyle, even if the song happened to be set in Arizona. The idea – of cruising down a highway and becoming entranced by a girl – could apply to young men in any state.

It was Frey who added the line, "It's a girl, my Lord, in a flatbed Ford, slowing down to take a look at me."

Frey and Henley began working on songs from the time the band came together. J.D. Souther and former roommate Jackson Browne joined in.

"It was a very protracted process," Souther recalled. "We were slow as molasses. Glenn would be walking around with a cigarette hanging out of his mouth, banging on a piano and keeping a groove going while Don and I tore our hair out and criticized everything."

Browne soon noted the differences between the two Eagles. "Glenn was this mercurial sort of flash," Browne said "He had boundless energy. Don was into being very analytical and methodical. He had the patience and the desire to hammer these songs into exactly what he meant. They made a really good combination."

John Boylan saw it this way: "His symbiosis with Frey was based on difference. Glenn brought Henley a sense of fun and commerciality, and Henley brought Glenn a more serious, intelligent, poetic way of looking at things."

Early on, all four Eagles wrote material. Bernie and Don teamed up for "Witchy Woman" and Leadon also offered up one of the highlights of his time with Dillard and Clark, the song he wrote with Clark, "Train Leaves Here This Morning". While "Witchy Woman" was Henley's only credit, Frey, besides his role in "Take It Easy", wrote "Chug All Night" and "Most Of Us Are Sad". Randy Meisner also wrote or co-wrote three songs that made the album.

But after "Witchy Woman" and "Take It Easy", the Eagles' biggest hit from their debut album was a languid, lilting song, "Peaceful Easy Feeling", which came from a singer-songwriter friend from San Diego, Jack Tempchin. When Frey and Souther, as Longbranch Pennywhistle, played the Candy Company club in San Diego they'd stay with Tempchin, who performed and ran the hootenannies at the club. And when Tempchin ventured to Hollywood to get in line for

the Monday open mikes at the Troubadour, he'd hang out at Frey and Souther's place, which he recalled as "a little pink bungalow in a hillside".

"Peaceful Easy Feeling", he said, was just one of his songs he'd been performing. He was playing it one day in Jackson Browne's apartment, below Frey and Souther's place, "and Glenn comes in and hears it… He whips out a cassette recorder. And the next day, the Eagles, who'd just been together for eight days, worked it up. Glenn comes back and plays me what they worked up, which was incredible."

Soon, the band was in London, where it was anything but peaceful, or easy. First, there was the matter of being in London. Johns liked working at Olympic Studios, Warner Bros. Records (Warner/Elektra/Atlantic, which was distributing Asylum's product) was willing to foot the bills, and that was that.

"So they packed us off to England," said Henley, "and stuck us in this little apartment, picked us up, took us to the studio, and then we'd go back to this little apartment and drink ourselves to sleep. Then we'd get up the next day and do it all over again."

Johns put the boys on a strict work schedule that went well into the night. He had a strict no-drugs policy in his studio, and he released them from Olympic so late that there was no time for any of London's famed pubs, or the female company they might have found there. It was as if they were in some form of protective custody.

In the studio, there was as much tension as music in the air. Johns seemed insistent that the Eagles' strong suit was the creation of peaceful, easy music. The Eagles wanted to rock out.

As Don remembered it, "Glyn thought we were a nice, country-rock, semi-acoustic band, and every time we wanted to rock 'n' roll, he could name a thousand British bands that could do it better."

"And he'd engineered the Stones on LPs like *Exile on Main Street,* so who the hell were we to be wanting to play rock 'n' roll? I mean he told us we couldn't play rock 'n' roll and to forget it. He was a complete tyrant. He would give us three chances to do a track or a vocal, and if that was the best we could do, then that was it." It was outright intimidating, said Henley: "You couldn't help but get emotional. We even cried a couple of times."

Had they been in Los Angeles, or working with another producer, the Eagles might have been able to find solace with friends, families or drugs. But stuck in London, with a warden in the guise of a record producer, they had no such escape. Henley recalls a couple of escape attempts: "Johns didn't like dope, so we'd have to sneak off to the bathroom to do dope."

Meisner and Frey rebelled against Johns' "no drugs in the studio" rule and what they perceived to be his authoritarian nature. "He pointed out a lot of bad habits in everybody," said Frey. "It's hard to be friends with someone who does that to you. It's a basic premise for friendship that you accept the threat that everybody else poses to you."

But Johns wasn't there to be friends; his job was to produce the best album possible from a band that was composed of two pros and two neophytes.

Jack Tempchin, the composer of "Peaceful Easy Feeling", stayed in touch with Frey. "Glenn's version is that Glyn Johns had been working with the Stones and he was frustrated working with people who had their own mind. He had the Eagles, this young band that didn't know what they were doing in the studio, and he made them rush through everything, and Glenn still feels that 'Peaceful Easy Feeling' is not really in tune.'"

Yet Johns' strict and structured ways worked. Within two weeks, the album was complete. Almost.

Back in Los Angeles, Geffen and Roberts decided that there wasn't enough Henley on the album, and had him go into a local studio with the band. He would sing lead on "Nightingale", a song Jackson Browne wrote about his affair with Laura Nyro. It was a solid, rocking tune, and it was one of only two lead vocals from Henley on the album. But it was a sign of his inevitable emergence from behind the drum kit to a lead singer's microphone.

It was the Browne-Frey composition "Take It Easy" that led off the record, with "Witchy Woman" as track two. And those were the first two cuts issued as singles. Both became hits, "Take It Easy" reaching No. 12 on the *Billboard* charts and the tom-tom-heavy "Witchy Woman" surpassing it,

PREVIOUS PAGE: The four band members looking a little worse for wear after a night spent out in the desert for the *Eagles* cover shoot.

RIGHT: Glyn Johns at work in the studio.

PREVIOUS PAGE: The band in London in the early days of the Eagles.

BELOW: The band had a good time in London while recording—sometimes at least.

RIGHT: A performance Dutch TV – *Popgala* – from 1973. The band toured Europe that year.

Just a month or so after the album's release, Glenn Frey was cautious as he spoke with Judith Sims, a Los Angeles correspondent for *Rolling Stone*. Reviewers had been kind, but Asylum Records – and the band – still needed to go out and promote the album. "We would not be disappointed if the record wasn't a success," he said, rather boldly – especially since he was doing the interview in David Geffen's office. "We liked the album … it's a statement of our backgrounds. The Eagles were conceived as a song-oriented band. It doesn't matter how good we can play if we address a piece of material that's inferior…"

Despite Frey's ambivalence about the album, it was enough of a success that Asylum hired Glyn Johns to oversee the follow-up. Once again, he required that the band travel to London –

this time to work at Island Studios, operated by Island Records in Notting Hill Gate.

They did, in early 1973. But in the months between the release of the first album and the beginning of the follow-up, the Eagles had changed.

Frey and Henley had assumed a co-leadership of the band, where, originally, it had been a four-way equal partnership. Said Henley, "When we formed the band, it was supposed to be one of those 'everybody's equal' affairs. We'd all sing and all write and so forth. But the fact is, people aren't all going to be able to do everything the same. It's just like on a football team… Some people quarterback, and some people block."

Leadon and Meisner may have been the better-known musicians, and were expected to take the lead roles, but both

were more players than performers. Meisner was shy, both off and on stage, and Leadon concentrated on his multitude of stringed instruments. Meantime, Henley and Frey became close friends, songwriting partners and, soon enough, the co-quarterbacks of the Eagles.

The songwriting began just days after their return from the London sessions for the first album. They started with "Desperado", which began as something else, much like "Yesterday", in Paul McCartney's mind, was originally "Scrambled Eggs".

Henley had only a fragment of the song, something he'd conjured around 1968. He remembers it having something to do with astrology, while Frey recalls that the original lyrics began with an astrological name: "Leo, my God, why don't you come to your senses…"

As Henley performed what he had of the song for Frey, singing and playing the piano, he said the music reminded him of Ray Charles and Stephen Foster: Southern Gothic. "Glenn leapt right on it," he said – "filled in the blanks and brought structure. And that was the beginning of our songwriting partnership… that's when we became a team."

The song came together after a post-Troubadour show jam involving Frey, Henley, Souther and Browne. Frey recalled, "That's when the idea came together about us doing an album of all the … antiheroes. 'James Dean' was going to be one song, and the Doolin-Dalton gang was going to be another. The idea became *Desperado*." He and Henley wrote the songs "Desperado" and "Tequila Sunrise" in the same week. Frey noted, about their budding songwriting relationship: "I think I brought him ideas and a lot of opinions; he brought me poetry — we were a good team."

The Doolin-Dalton Gang were train robbers in the Oklahoma territory in the 1890s. How did they get to share a sentence with the 1950s actor James Dean? (His song would wind up on the album after *Desperado*).

The idea of rock stars being equivalent to the outlaws of the Wild West in the 1890s came from a photo book Glenn had received from fellow fledgling songwriter Ned Doheny. The book told of the exploits of the Doolin-Dalton Gang of train robbers.

The gang wound up caught and killed by lawmen. That didn't faze Frey. "We sort of saw ourselves as living outside the law, just like the guys we were writing about," he said. The recording session proceeded, and, he recalled, "Halfway through, we realized it was holding together. The whole outlaw and rock star idea that we were trying to get across was working."

"Not outlaws in the sense of outlaws today," Henley noted. "Maybe more of a Robin Hood thing..."

Henley had more than cowboys and outlaws in mind. Even though the Eagles were still on their climb to the top, he was already becoming disenchanted with the business and with the cost of success in pop music.

"It's sad when you learn what the rock and roll business is all about," he said. "That's basically what the *Desperado* album deals with. With growing up, and learning what the real world is about, and learning that there are certain compromises and sacrifices you have to make. In other words, you have to do what everyone else wants you to do for a while. And during that time you have to maintain your identity, remember who you are and what you want to do."

He told another reporter: "I think we knew early on that fame was a fleeting thing... that you get up just to get torn down eventually, and that this is a fickle business. That's what that album was all about, you know: that we would all be hung sooner or later. Or hang ourselves."

In making a concept album so early in their career, the Eagles were going out on a limb. Frey said he was inspired by the Who's *A Quick One*. "It was sort of this rock-opera concept-album idea floating around..."

Others in the band jumped aboard. Said Leadon, "We grew up wanting to be cowboys, so much so that we actually wanted to act that out. The album was our chance to do that."

Or, more accurately, the album cover was their opportunity to play cowboys. As they did for the Eagles' first recording, the band teamed with photographer Henry Diltz and designer Gary Burden. This time, there'd be no peyote party in the high desert. This time, it'd be a shootout. That's what the Eagles staged, on what looked to be a Western movie soundstage in the hills of Malibu. Along with roadies and pals (including Souther and Browne), they portrayed bank robbers who, as Burden put it, "come to town and stop working and take the easy way... and rob a bank... and in the process they get killed."

The action, captured by Diltz on a Super 8 camera, was too much for Warner Bros. But photos, looking authentically vintage, of the Eagles as outlaw gunslingers graced the cover. And on the back, there they were, captured and killed, lying together on a street.

The album itself was an artistic triumph. Even if the concept didn't come together for Frey until they were halfway through, the end result was a strong musical statement about life in the Wild West – whether it was the late 19th Century or the early Seventies. With elegance, Johns and the Eagles stated and re-stated the themes, of the Doolin-Dalton saga and of the Everyman as a desperado. Henley's plaintive, soulful voice came to the fore, again and again. But there was also Bernie Leadon, reminding listeners that country rock came from country & western, as he performed banjo, mandolin and dobro on his song "Twenty-One". Randy Meisner weighed in with a yowling lead vocal on his composition with Henley and Frey, "A Certain Kind of Fool". "I just got in at the last minute of that album with that one," he said. Amidst Henley and Frey's partnership, he said, "it was kind of hard to be heard. I had a riff, and they helped me finish it."

The one song that evoked the Eagles of the first album was "Tequila Sunrise", an ode not so much to the theme of the album as to the sub-theme of life as an Eagle in Los Angeles, where Sauza Conmemorativo was the drink of choice for many. As Henley recalled, Frey was concerned that the tequila reference might be heard as a cliché, but he advised his partner to look at it from another point of view: "You've been drinking straight tequila all night, and the sun is coming up!" Frey relented, and Henley exulted, years later: "That's one song I don't get tired of. 'Take another shot of courage' refers

RIGHT: Relations were sometimes strained with the band as they stayed together in an apartment in London, England while recording.

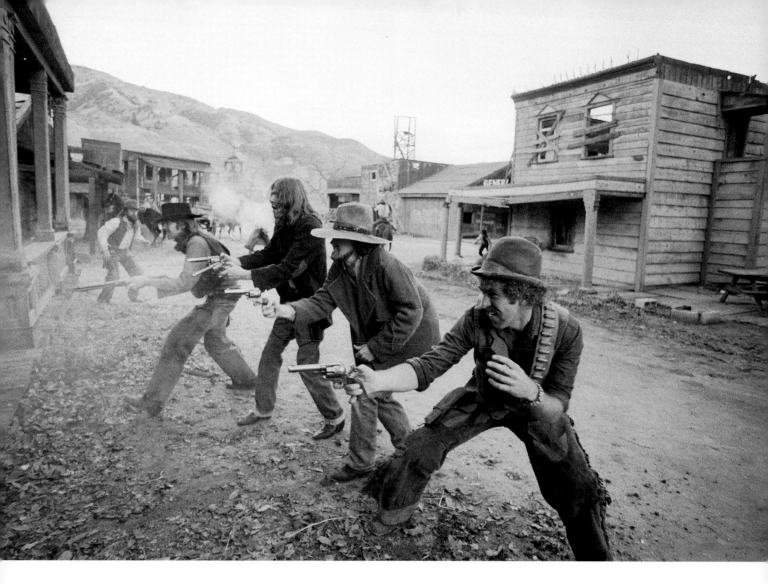

to tequila, because we used to call it 'instant courage.' We very much wanted to talk to the ladies, but we often didn't have the nerve, so we'd drink a couple of shots and suddenly it was, 'Howdy, ma'am.'"

There was little "Howdy, ma'am" going on in London, where, under Glyn Johns' rule, the band took only four weeks to record the album. They left London satisfied. Randy Meisner, for one, was to describe *Desperado* as "one of the best albums we ever made" because "it was focused... we had the concept from start to finish." He was proud of it, but added that David Geffen and Elliot Roberts weren't quite as thrilled: "They thought it was the biggest mistake we ever made... and the record label didn't want it at all."

Frey recalled, "There were some people who weren't too happy. All they could think was: 'They made a goddamn cowboy record! Where's 'Witchy Woman'? Where's 'Take It Easy'? 'Chrissakes! They made a fuckin' cowboy record!'"

The worrywarts, as it turns out, were right. *Desperado* reached No. 41 on the album charts in 1973 and produced

not one hit single, although the title track received additional exposure through Linda Ronstadt's recording of it. Yet although "Tequila Sunrise" didn't make the Top 40, reaching only No. 64, it was a staple of FM rock radio in 1973, when the "album rock" format stood apart from Top 40 and had a power all its own.

After the album had proven to be a commercial failure, Glyn Johns accused Asylum Records of "not being on the case". At the time, Asylum Records was merging with Elektra, its older sister label, and Geffen was put in charge of the new company. One of his target signings was Bob Dylan. Geffen, said Johns, "was more involved in trying to sign Dylan than putting any kind of support behind the album. It's disgraceful that it wasn't a monster-hit album. It should have taken the world by storm."

Desperado would become a million-seller, in time, as the Eagles became superstars and fans went in search of previous efforts. In fact, by 2001, the RIAA had certified the album as double platinum, signifying sales of two million copies. By then, it had also been enshrined in the Grammy Hall of Fame,

PREVIOUS PAGE: The photo shoot for the album
cover of *Desperado*…

LEFT: … involved a lot of dressing up, playing with
guns and getting the right feel for the subject.

BELOW: Back in the USA, Glenn Frey shares a joke
with a friend.

75

recognizing its "qualitative or historical significance".

As Frey noted, "It's a record and concept that has stood the test of time; it's gotten better as time has gone on. As a whole piece, it's a well-recognized concept album."

And, despite the Eagles' enmity toward the rock press, *Rolling Stone* recognized its merits, as well. Reviewer Paul Gambaccini, a New England native who had moved to London, where he served as a correspondent for the magazine, wrote: "With their second consecutive job well done, the Eagles are on a winning streak."

Gambaccini didn't hear *Desperado* as a concept album. To him, it was simply a collection of good tunes. Midway through the recording sessions, he noted, the Eagles and Johns discovered that the tracks could be placed in a specific order, and tell a story.

Gambaccini thought he heard three hits: "Out of Control" ("a hard rock number with instrumental overtones of the Who"), "Desperado" (featuring Henley's "voice of experience"), and "Saturday Night." Long before Henley would compose "The End of the Innocence," he was writing, Gambaccini said, about lost lovers, past times, and "the never-to-be-regained innocence."

These were themes that would become familiar in the Eagles' songbook, and they indicated that the band members were growing – fast. Or, as country-rock historian John Einarson wrote years later, "The record shows the maturity and the stronger sense of lyricism the four songwriters had developed since their first release." He continued: "It stands as a high-water mark, the culmination of the vision of four musicians raised on cowboy lore and western movies. *Desperado* was as much a product of image as substance, though the substance was worthy."

And it was only the Eagles' sophomore effort. As fine as it was – especially in hindsight (and sound) – the relative lack of success only put another charge into the band.

As Meisner put it: "I don't think there were any kind of feelings in the band that, 'Gosh, we did the wrong thing.' It was like, 'Okay, let's go on and do the next one now.'"

5

ON THE BRINK

———◦⧖◦———

Don Henley was prescient. Along with financial rewards, becoming a successful rock

band brought sacrifices, compromises, and pressures, within and outside of the band.

They now had to deal with business complications from agents, managers and, especially,

the record company.

The rewards themselves, however, were almost overwhelming.

With money came the ability to rent their own homes, and Henley and Frey wound up as neighbors in Laurel Canyon, with Frey's place, at Ridpath and Kirkwood, coming to be known as "The Kirkwood Casino and Health Club." Friends learned the routine, beginning with dinner at Dan Tana's, drinks at the Troub (and maybe a show), and then up to the fitness club for beer, booze, poker (or basketball in daylight on weekends), drugs, women, and general fun and mayhem.

But they did report to their day jobs, as rock stars. Frey and Henley wrote songs at their homes, and they soon began to compile tracks for their next album.

The Eagles agreed to work with Glyn Johns again – and in London again – but, after convening at Olympic Studios, in fall of 1973, they continued to do battle over their musical ideas. Johns thought the band had done well with its country-rock sound; the boys continued to press for more rock and less country.

But not all the Eagles were in agreement. While Henley and Frey wanted to rock out more, with Frey expressing an interest in injecting more R&B sounds into the music, Meisner and Leadon weren't so sure. Their ambivalence was driven, in part, by an uncertainty, and anxiety, over their evolving roles in the band. With Henley and Frey assuming a *de facto* leadership position, the other two had to work hard to get in a song or a lead vocal of their own.

Arguments began to flare in the studio, and, where the debut album had taken two weeks and *Desperado* about twice that, things were getting exponentially worse. After six weeks of work, they had produced only two tracks: "Best of My Love" (credited to Henley, Frey and Souther), and "You Never Cry Like a Lover", written by Henley with Souther.

Henley was to reveal that the in-studio battles had been going since he and Frey had grabbed the reins on *Desperado*. "The only two people in this group who tend to think alike are Glenn and me," he said, "and we've always wanted every song to be the best that it could be. We didn't want any filler. So there have been plenty of fights."

Producer Johns, he said, accused him and Frey of wanting to rewrite lyrics composed by Meisner and Leadon. No, said Henley. Well, not exactly. The guys could write what they wanted. "It's just how they say it," Henley explained. "When somebody hears a bad song, they're not gonna say, 'So-and-so wrote a weak song.' They're gonna say, 'There's a shitty song on the Eagles album.' It reflects on everybody."

But who's to judge a "bad song"? "I suppose it's a matter of taste," Henley conceded.

Seeking diplomacy, Henley praised Leadon and Meisner's playing. But as for songwriting: "We've just taken it upon ourselves that this is our department. Maybe we're full of shit but I think we've proven ourselves. We recognize the fact that those guys have got a need to say something and if we can help them say it better, then I think everybody's better off. It's not a matter of credit or money or any of that stuff. We've been splitting the publishing equally from the beginning."

Besides each other, the band also had issues with London. "We couldn't think over there; we couldn't create," said Henley. And being cooped up in the studio and the apartment didn't help any. As Meisner put it, "You can't settle things out if you're not alone in your own home."

And, more than Olympic Studios and London, they still had problems with their producer. "The main objection we had to Glyn was that he considers that he has a certain sound," said Leadon. "In other words, the producer is the filter for the band to get on tape. He shapes it. Glyn has what he considers his stamp that he puts on something that you do. Echo is part of this. We figured some tunes deserved that much echo and some deserve less. We tried to work it out, but it wasn't really happening."

One morning, in October, the band reported to Olympic Studios. Instead of getting to work, they told Johns that they were going to try another producer. The Eagles then put together a tour that kept them occupied for a couple of months. They would pick things up in Los Angeles.

Johns agreed that the last sessions were "a disaster area," but claimed that he was blameless. "There were a lot of hang-ups, individually and with each other," he said. "But what it boils down to is they weren't ready to make another record. I certainly got frustrated on some occasions because they wouldn't grab the situation and get on it with. I don't believe in kid-gloving artists."

However, when the Eagles reconvened in Los Angeles after their tour, they discovered that their business environment was changing – and not necessarily for the better.

David Geffen, who had signed them to his label, Asylum, and to his management company, was moving at warp speed. In October, he'd received an offer he found difficult to refuse. It came from Steve Ross, head of Warner Communications, the umbrella company for Warner Bros. Records and sister labels including Atlantic, Elektra, Nonesuch and Reprise. Atlantic Records had been distributing Asylum Records' product. Now, Ross wanted to buy it and merge it with Elektra, paying Geffen

Henley and Frey wanted to rock out more, with Frey expressing an interest in injecting more R&B sounds

PREVIOUS PAGE: And then there were five: Leadon, Frey, Henley, new boy Don Felder and Meisner.

BELOW: Henley, Frey, Felder, Leadon and Meisner.
RIGHT: Don Henley takes a moment…

$7m in cash and stocks, with the provision that he run the merged label.

Geffen had formed a management company with Elliot Roberts, with an all-star roster including Joni Mitchell, Neil Young, and Crosby, Stills & Nash, as well as the Eagles. Geffen-Roberts Management had also taken in an ambitious young man from Illinois named Irving Azoff, who was managing singer-songwriter Dan Fogelberg and rocker Joe Walsh. Geffen soon left the managing to Roberts, an associate, John Hartmann, and Azoff while he tended to the record company. He was on his way to becoming, ultimately vice chairman of Warner Bros. film studios.

None of this impressed the Eagles.

"It's the old sauna story," said Henley. "Glenn was at David Geffen's house one day, and Geffen told him, 'I want to keep Asylum Records really small. I'll never have more artists than I can fit in this sauna.' Then, all of a sudden, he was signing people right and left."

They felt even less special when Geffen left their management in the hands of Roberts, who'd handled Mitchell

and her peers. The Eagles wanted someone closer to their own, younger ages. "We were always the young guys down there. Nobody paid much attention to us."

Irving Azoff did. As a college kid in Illinois, he'd become a booking agent for various bands in the Midwest, including the Cryan' Shames, Shades of Blue and the James Gang. After moving to Los Angeles in 1972, he connected with Joe Walsh of the James Gang, and with a singer-songwriter he had met in Illinois and wanted to manage: Dan Fogelberg. He did, and he soon established a style all of his own. Standing five feet three inches short, Azoff was a fireball of brains and bravado, employing a blend of high volume, threats and, occasionally, lies to get his way.

One day, at Geffen-Roberts' offices, he was asked to take care of a problem involving the Eagles – something to do with a limo not showing up at an airport. He was an avid Eagles fan, and he quickly took care of business. He began traveling with the band, proving himself as adept at hotel-room destructions and other pranks as any rock star.

After looking into the Eagles' books and deciding that they could be doing much better – especially with Asylum

PREVIOUS PAGE: The new five-piece band about to jet off in August 1974.

LEFT: Glenn Frey is on top of the world; Don Henley takes the weight off his shoulders, circa 1974.

BELOW: Leadon, Frey (back to camera) and Felder live on stage in the USA.

85

Don got his first guitar from a kid who was willing to give it up in trade for some cherry bombs and firecrackers he and Jerry got from their uncle. The guitar was in horrible condition, but he worked with it until his father helped him get a Silvertone archtop from Sears & Roebuck. He devoted all his spare time to it, and he soon graduated to an electric guitar with a Fender amp. He was 11 years old.

He began playing in public and at 15 formed a band, the Continentals, which played teen dances and junior high schools. Among the kids who joined the band for a few dances was another teenager; a singer and guitarist named Stephen Stills.

Felder also worked at a newly-opened music shop and began giving guitar lessons, earning money to pay for a new Fender Stratocaster he had eyed in the window. One of his star pupils, he said, was a kid called Tom Petty, three years Don's junior and a member of a band called the Rucker Brothers. Like Stills, he was on his way to other places and bigger things.

In 1964, Bernie Leadon moved into Gainesville, from San Diego, and the two became friends and bandmates. (One of Bernie's younger brothers, Tom, wound up in a band with Petty. It was called Mudcrutch – the core of the Heartbreakers.)

Felder and Leadon's band, the Maundy Quintet, got steady work, even landing a couple of engagements in New York. They composed songs and recorded a couple of singles. Felder was in love with Susan, a girl from Boston. Then, in 1967, Leadon left for California, Susan went home to Boston, and the Maundy Quintet disbanded.

Moving to New York, Felder next joined Flow, which, he said, "specialized in freeform jazz-rock and were heavily into pot". After recording one album, Felder moved to Boston, where he reunited with Susan, played R&B in a club, and had day jobs in recording studios, playing, writing jingles and helping to book other musicians.

On the Brink

Now and again, he'd hear from Leadon, encouraging him to move out to Los Angeles, where he'd found plentiful work – work that was a bit more substantial than writing jingles for local car dealerships. Bernie had already played behind Linda Ronstadt and been part of the Flying Burrito Brothers. Stills had become a star, with Buffalo Springfield and, now, with Crosby, Stills & Nash. Meantime, Felder got married and stayed in Boston.

In the summer of 1972, Leadon and Felder saw each other again. Leadon was now in the Eagles, and they were playing at Boston University. Felder got to meet the rest of the band and, in their dressing room, jammed on guitar with Leadon. Afterwards, he remembered, "Frey came over and placed a hand on my shoulder. 'Man, you're good,' he said. 'You should come to L.A. We could use a few more players like you out there.'" Two months later, he and Susan packed up, rented a U-Haul and said goodbye to their friends. And hello, finally, to California.

In Los Angeles, he and his talent found work within the Troubadour/Eagles/Geffen circles. Geffen managed a singer-songwriter named David Blue, and Felder was hired for his touring band. Heard on tour by Graham Nash, he was asked to do double duty, for both Blue and for the duo of Crosby & Nash. One night, they were joined on stage by Felder's erstwhile Gainesville band mate, Stephen Stills. For a moment, he marveled, it was Crosby, Stills, Nash & Felder.

Now, in January 1974, the Eagles needed him. "Glenn called and asked me to come play a slide solo on a track called 'Good Day in Hell'," he was to explain. It was a perfect showcase for Felder's sizzling style, giving the band a new, more incendiary edge. They wanted more, and the next day, Frey called again – this time to invite him to join the band. "Sure," Felder replied. He agreed to report back to the studio to help finish the album, hung up, and turned to Susan, now pregnant with their first child.

"Wow," he managed.

"There were only four Eagles," said Frey, "and I could never foresee that framework actually changing. But I saw no one who could fit in as completely as Don does. He's definitely the fifth Eagle."

The next day, Felder entered the Record Plant – now as a full-fledged Eagle – and was greeted and welcomed into the fold by each of the guys. The last one to approach him was Leadon, who gave him a hug and then whispered in his ear: "Don't say I didn't warn you."

His words were telling. Felder was not boarding a happy ship. As he told a television reporter, years later: "When I first joined the band, I thought I'd joined a band that had just broken up."

In his autobiography *Heaven And Hell: My Life in the Eagles 1974–2001*, he explained: "Bernie was bouncing off the wall and Randy was threatening to quit." And, he said, the tension was present every day when the band was recording.

Henley agreed. "Glenn and I assumed this bulldozer attitude of, 'We ain't gonna put up with any weaknesses,'" he said. "'Every song's gonna be great!' There was a lot of fighting."

Out of all the craziness came *On the Border*, a mash of all things Eagles, minus any over-arching concept. With Felder on board, the band rocked on "Already Gone", the leftover "James Dean", "Good Day in Hell" and the bluegrass-hued "Midnight Flyer" with Meisner on lead vocals and an arrangement clearly influenced by Gram Parsons' "Ooh Las Vegas". Meisner also sang lead vocals on "Is It True", his lone songwriting credit on the album.

Leadon wrote and sang "My Man", with references to Parsons, who had died of a drug overdose in Joshua Tree in September 1973, just weeks before the Eagles began work on the album. "Good Day in Hell", a Frey-Henley composition, was also about Parsons. Frey and Henley also teamed up with another ex-Burrito Brother, Leadon, for the title track. As they had on their first album, they also took in songs from friends like Souther and Browne and included outsiders' tunes like "Ol' '55" by Tom Waits.

"Already Gone", co-written with Jack Tempchin, who had composed "Peaceful Easy Feeling", barely cracked the Top 40, peaking at No. 32. No matter. For the band, the song signified the change from Glyn Johns, the intimidating taskmaster, to the much looser Bill Szymczyk. Henley, who'd been driven to tears by Johns, said of Szymczyk: "He was like a soul mate. We got along really well; he'd get just as high and crazy as we were."

The good times found their way into tracks such as "Already Gone". Said Frey: "The 'All right, nighty-night' at the end of the song was sort of typical of the spontaneous feeling we wanted

LEFT: Randy Meisner is interviewed while on tour with the Eagles in London, circa 1974.

OVERLEAF: Walter Yetnikoff (of CBS Records), Irving Azoff (Eagles manager), and Joe Smith in Beverly Hills.

on our records. I was much more comfortable in the studio with Bill, and he was more than willing to let everyone stretch a bit. 'Already Gone' is me being happier; it's me being free."

Ironically, the song that sprung the Eagles loose from their country-rock anchor was conceived as a country song. At least, that's what Tempchin was trying for. "Robb Strandlin, a country musician, was my buddy in San Diego," he said. "One night we got drunk at the Back Door, wrote the song in about 20 minutes and went and played it. A tape turned up, and Glenn heard it, and a few years later he called me and said: 'You know that country song you wrote? I think it'd make a good rock song.' He held the phone up to the speaker, and *whammo!*"

But the album's biggest single would be a ballad. "Best of My Love", a gorgeous love song by Henley, Frey and Souther, gave the Eagles their first US No. 1 single in early 1975. It was one of the two songs Johns had produced, and it was the kind of tune Johns thought that the band did best: sweet, smooth, country harmonies.

The song, Henley said, dated back to the Troubadour and Dan Tana's, to when the Eagles were nothing. As Henley recalled: "That was the period when there were all these great-looking girls who didn't really want to have anything to do with us. We were just scruffy new kids who had no calling card. We wanted the girls to like us, but we had all the immature emotions that young men have – jealousy, envy, frustration, lust, insecurity: the lot. At the same time, however, we were also becoming quite adept at brushing off girls who showed any interest in us: 'If you want to be with me, I can't possibly give you the time of day. I want that girl over there who couldn't care less if I live or die.'"

Propelled by "Best of My Love", *On the Border* reached No. 17 on *Billboard*'s Top 40 albums listing and stayed in the chart for 24 weeks. Their debut had only a seven-week stay. *Desperado*, of course, had been shut out.

Frey thought the album deserved its success. "*On the Border* is easily the best sounding recording we've ever made," he said. "We're starting to learn how to become recording artists, which is different from learning how to be members of a band." Meisner agreed. "Before, when we were finishing one album, we were already working on another," he said. "But with *On the Border*, I think the band had finally reached a real good creative place."

The critics generally agreed. Let's look at *Rolling Stone*, since the Eagles would single out that magazine as being particularly abusive. The publication, still based in San Francisco, had given the first two albums rave notices, from critics working out of Los Angeles and London. For *On the Border*, the assignment went to Janet Maslin in Boston. She opened with a couple of salvos, about how "the Eagles' point of view toward their material varies so wildly that it's hard to believe even they take it seriously," and how jarring she found the contrast between the tenderness of "My Man", Leadon's tribute to Parsons, and the "jovial necrophilia" of "James Dean". She thought the addition of Felder resulted in "too many intrusive guitar parts" and "too many solos that smack of gratuitous heaviness". In adding Felder, the Eagles had sought a heavier sound. They got it, apparently.

Maslin also noted that Frey and Henley, by sharing vocals on "Ol' '55," rendered the reading of the song less personal. And, of Meisner's "Midnight Flyer", she suggested, "Randy Meisner probably shouldn't be singing leads at all." Frey and Leadon sounded OK, she wrote, but she found Henley's "raw, strained sound" more interesting than that of his mates.

The Eagles, she said, were no longer outlaws. "They're thinking Top 40, and they now do it better than ever." *On the Border*, she concluded, "is a tight and likeable collection" that was "good enough to make up in high spirits what it lacks in purposefulness. And that might be even a fair trade if the Eagles would rein in their hit-making instincts and channel their energies into projects less easily within their grasp."

So: Not a rave, but not a slam, either. Maslin's was a balanced assessment, concluding with a challenge that, whether or not they took it seriously, the Eagles would take to heart. It was just one of those albums.

> *We were just scruffy new kids who had no calling card. We wanted the girls to like us.*

6

THE THRILL IS GONE

On the Border was kind of a tease, not unlike the women depicted in song by the Eagles.

The album would go on to sell well, but initial indicators, such as singles, gave the band

mixed signals. Frey already knew that the Eagles' strength lay not on Top 40 radio but on

album rock stations. Still, all artists lived for those radio hits, those tunes that, like "Take

It Easy", came to be heard everywhere. From *On the Border*, the first single,

"Already Gone", appeared to already be a goner. Issued ahead of the album,

it would barely break into the Top 40.

Fleeting and broken romances became fodder for many of the songs he would write, and when Rodkin left early in 1975, with the Eagles' next album underway, the songs flowed.

By now, one of those love-torn songs of his, "Best of My Love", was moving up the Top 40 charts. Asylum didn't release it as a single until November 1974, nine months after *On the Border* had come out. The ballad, one of the two surviving tracks from the Glyn Johns sessions, followed two other singles, both rockers: "Already Gone" and "James Dean".

It was the slow song that made it, hitting No. 1 for one week in late February. The Eagles were not about to get into a ballads groove. "We were looking to go further and further away from the country-rock influence and more towards a rock 'n' roll influence," said producer Szymczyk. "We were looking at it being a little more electric."

After his break-up with Loree Rodkin and before he hooked up with Stevie Nicks in late 1975, Henley moved into Frey's house, on Briarcrest Lane, high up in Laurel Canyon, where they did a lot of – well, everything. Henley explained the setting and the routine to writer and film director Cameron Crowe, in the context of writing one of his and Frey's most popular songs.

"'Lyin' Eyes'," he said, "is one of the songs written when Glenn and I were roommates in a house we rented up in Trousdale. It was built in 1942 by the actress Dorothy Lamour. Glenn and I lived at opposite ends of the house and we actually converted a music room to a full-on recording studio. The house was located at the highest point on the hill and we had a 360° panorama. In the daytime, we could see snowcapped peaks to the east and the blue Pacific to the west. At night, the twinkling lights of the city below were breathtaking. We had some great times up there."

The house, Frey said, was where they composed "One of These Nights", "Lyin' Eyes", "Take It to the Limit" and "After the Thrill Is Gone".

"One of These Nights", said Henley, was a nod to their love of rhythm & blues music, of Al Green in Memphis and the work of the producers Gamble & Huff out of

LEFT: Bernie Leadon during a quiet moment on stage, circa 1974. In this shot he is pictured with a pedal steel guitar, another of his instruments.

ABOVE: Multi-instrumentalist Leadon on stage again, this time playing six-string guitar. By 1975 he would no longer be a member of the band.

6 The Thrill is Gone

However, he was with the band for one of their biggest gigs ever, when the Eagles performed at the Midsummer Madness concert at Wembley, a football stadium just outside London, on June 21, 1975, before 72,000 people. Felder, who had missed the California Jam, made this one. "It was awesome," he said. "The place and the people just made us high. We didn't need anything else."

It didn't hurt that they were riding high on several hit records. Following such acts as Rufus and Joe Walsh (another Irving Azoff client), they were billed third, under headliner Elton John and the Beach Boys. The Beach Boys were said to have dominated the show, but, according to Andy Childs, editor of the UK magazine *Zigzag*: "The Eagles blew our heads apart and put them back together again! They were astounding!" In a long but tight 15-song set, they proved that, five men strong, they were ready for the big stage.

By fall, Leadon was feeling better – or, at least, he was saying he was. "My attitude toward the band is pretty good these days," he told Cameron Crowe in *Rolling Stone*, which featured the Eagles on its cover in a September issue. "We've all grown a lot. Everybody realizes this is a good opportunity to get some bucks and also, man, I think the music is worth something. There's so much bullshit

in the pop world. So much of it is just… sexually oriented. That's a form of escape. I like to think our band is more than that… In the meantime, I just don't want to succumb to the comforts of an affluent society and say, 'OK, this is swell, I give in.'"

He was talking about such rock star accoutrements as limousines. Using them, he said, "It feels like you're thumbing your nose at your audience." Still, he went along for the rides. It would have been strange speeding away from a concert venue in a motorhome.

But he was an unhappy passenger. In the studio, despite getting his song or two in, he groused, along with Meisner and Felder, about their decreased songwriting credits (and, they feared, publishing royalties). He was a lone voice fighting for the Eagles to include country sounds in the music. During the *One of These Nights* sessions, when he tired of the fighting, he'd just leave, for days on end, to go surfing. Leadon, Felder said, was the first of the Eagles to turn his back on the shenanigans of the Third Encore and to embrace a healthier lifestyle.

While the Eagles dealt with the Leadon issue, they celebrated their biggest-selling album yet, as *One of These Nights* hit No. 1. But they couldn't help letting the critics spoil their

BELOW: Legendary English singer Elton John appears on stage with Henley, Meisner, Felder, Leadon and Frey, circa 1975.

RIGHT: Glenn Frey plays another concert while on tour in the USA. The constant touring was proving to be a drain to some members of the band.

fun. In his memoirs, *Heaven and Hell*, Felder wrote that in the same issue of *Rolling Stone* that featured Crowe's friendly cover story on the Eagles, the editors ran a negative review of the album, and that Henley had sent the magazine a scathing letter.

In fact, the review in *Rolling Stone* was in August 1975, a month before the cover story, and, although the critic, Stephen Holden, was a New Yorker, it was by no means a critical assassination. It even ran under the headline "Sweet and Sexy Songs from L.A."

In the review, Holden heard a likeable "sweetness" in the band's songs – even in their most pessimistic ones. That sweetness worked well, he said, with excellent arrangements and musicianship, as well as Frey, Henley and Meisner's vocal harmonies. The result: a musical evocation of "everything gratifying that people would like to fantasize about L.A." Holden singled out "One of These Nights" for praise. The harmonies were both tough and tight, and he liked Don Felder's "muscular" guitar work.

Holden did have problems with "Journey of the Sorcerer" ("a trite after-thought, poorly sung"), but so did all of the Eagles except for Leadon. What got Henley's Afro wigged out, no doubt, was Holden's conclusion that the Eagles' latest was "not a great album," that "they lack an outstanding singer," and that "while many of their tunes are pretty, none are eloquent." And "for all their worldly perceptiveness, the Eagles' lyrics never transcend Hollywood slickness."

Still, Holden was compelled to quote a few lines, from "Take It to the Limit" and "After the Thrill is Gone". In the latter, the Eagles ask what happens when dreams come true and they're not what they'd expected, and wind up doing "the same old dances in the same old shoes / You don't care about winning but you don't want to lose."

That tune, said Frey, was "a lot of self-examination". Said Henley: "As exciting as the whole Eagles thing was at times, some of the luster was beginning to wear off. We were combining our personal and professional lives in song."

LEFT: Don Henley on the drums, during a concert in Anaheim, CA in late 1975.   ABOVE: On the runway, preparing to fly. Note Bernie Leadon's lack of footwear!

" *As exciting as the whole Eagles thing was at times, some of the luster was beginning to wear off.* "

7

HEY, JOE

───────◆◆◆───────

The announcement of Bernie Leadon's departure from the Eagles came in December 1975. The truth was, he was already gone long before then. Leadon has said that he'd been thinking about leaving as long as two years before he finally did. And then came one day or night in December 1975, in Cincinnati or some southern city, in a hotel bar or in Frey's room – it all depends on who's trying to remember the story …

He soon left the James Gang, saying he was composing music with more textures and harmonies than a trio could handle. He was also disenchanted with his band mates' response to their success: "Everybody started buying big cars. The emphasis came off good music and creating; that was all left behind. The money was great, but I felt like a whore." After a final tour, he left in November 1971 and took a six-month sabbatical from music. He moved to Colorado: "I was so sick of it all. I just got drunk a lot, ran around the mountains and waited till I felt creative again."

Walsh returned to music with a solo album, *Barnstorm*, which displayed his softer side: "I was thinking I was going to be James Taylor." His fans weren't buying it, and he fell into a funk. "The IRS was auditing me three years running," he said. "My manager didn't care."

Walsh turned to Irving Azoff, who he'd met at a James Gang gig in Lake Geneva, Wisconsin. Azoff was then a booking agent but happily agreed to try managing Walsh. "That means I don't have to be an agent any more," he said. Next, Walsh beefed up his band, also called Barnstorm. It included drummer Joe Vitale, who would also figure in the Eagles' future. Walsh's 1973 album *The Smoker You Drink, the Player You Get*, produced by Szymczyk and including "Rocky Mountain Way", was a smash. So was a 1975 album, *So What*.

By then, he had become buddies with various Eagles. *The Smoker…* included a song, "Falling Down", that he wrote with Henley. Henley, Frey and Meisner sang on two other songs, "Turn to Stone" and "Help Me Through the Night". Walsh knew all about their concerns about Bernie Leadon.

"We had talked to Joe before Bernie left," Frey told *Melody Maker*. "And his attitude was, if Leadon left, we should give him a call."

When the call came, it was good timing for Walsh. "After a couple of albums by myself, I was starting to feel drained, alone and in need of feedback. I just did not want to have

ABOVE: Glenn Frey, circa 1976. The long hair was much in vogue at that time, not long after the departure of Bernie Leadon.

ABOVE: Don Felder photographed around the same time. Felder was out of the band by 2001, an acrimonious separation.

ABOVE: Eagles with extras, left to right: Don Henley, Randy Meisner, Don Felder, Dan Fogelberg, Jackson Browne, Joe Walsh, Linda Ronstadt and Kenny Edwards.

OVERLEAF: Eagles Don Felder and Joe Walsh (left and right) with Linda Ronstadt and California Governor Jerry Brown between them. May 14, 1976.

to keep rehearsing a band and putting out all these intense amounts of energy. And musically I felt I could relate to these other four guys."

He was right, but the announcement still shocked fans and the media. They didn't see the hard-rocking Walsh fitting in with a band that, both on stage and in recordings, seemed not only mellow in sound but also disciplined in their playing. They were macho in their lyrics but they did little rock-fueled strutting. Joe Walsh was a strutter, which didn't sit particularly well with Henley. Early on, the drummer advised the newcomer that the Eagles did not "perform" on stage. The audience was there for the music, not theatrics.

Walsh, of course, was there for both. He agreed to tone himself down. But, once in the lights, he couldn't help himself. Nor could the audience. From his first shows with the Eagles, Walsh established himself as the crowd's favorite.

Henley, who had just begun to emerge from the drum riser to take his rightful position, stage front, as the band's primary voice, was less than thrilled. So was Felder, who now shared lead-guitar duties with a far flashier player. But Frey was delighted: "The guitar playing in the band, and the musical platforms, are much more to my liking now."

The critics liked him, too. The moment Walsh joined them, wrote John Swenson in his book *Headliners*, "The Eagles were,

> " *We had talked to Joe before Bernie left, and his attitude was, if Leadon left, we should give him a call.* "

in effect, an entirely new band. They'd already rejected their identity as a country rock band... but Walsh turned them whole hog into a rock 'n' roll outfit." They offered each other perfect complements, Swenson said: the Eagles gave Walsh's songs the intricate harmonies he sought, "while Walsh added a toughness and purpose to the Eagles' ensemble sound that provided the band with a decided direction at a time when they were looking for a new purpose".

With Walsh aboard, the band resumed touring. At the same time, they were working on the album that would be their most critically successful: *Hotel California*. But it was a long, estranged trip, slowed down by songwriters' blocks, intra-band rivalries and in-studio battles, road-trip hangovers and various ailments. Henley developed a stomach disorder that drove him to go on a Mylanta kick – and not because he liked the taste of the pain reliever. It got to the point that in February 1976, an exasperated Warner Bros., faced with no Eagles product since the previous June, and with the band yet to even enter the studios again, issued a compilation, *Eagles: Their Greatest Hits 1971–1975*, on Elektra/Asylum. This riled the band. Although they had, in fact, scored eight hit singles in just over three years, they thought a "greatest hits" record was a stretch.

Henley called the album a ploy by their label to make money without investing production costs. "It's that typical corporate thinking," he said. "All the record company was worried about was their quarterly reports. They didn't give a shit whether the greatest hits album was good or not; they just wanted product."

Henley's grumbling was quickly drowned out by the sound of cash registers at record stores. The collection sold an astounding million copies within a week, Felder recalls. There was no denying that the Eagles had become a superstar act. Early in 1976, "Take It to the Limit", the Meisner showcase, reached No. 4 on *Billboard* and stayed in the pop chart for the next 14 weeks. In February, the National Academy of Recording Arts and Sciences (NARAS), whose members vote for the annual Grammy Awards, named the Eagles winners in the category of Best Pop Vocal Performance by a Duo, Group or Chorus for "Lyin' Eyes".

The Eagles, who, like most rock artists, perceived the Grammys to be hopelessly behind the times and devoted to conservative

RIGHT: Keeping the country look: Felder, Walsh, Henley, Meisner and Frey, circa 1976.

7   Hey, Joe

pop music, didn't bother to attend the ceremonies in Los Angeles. They had returned not long ago from a short tour in Japan. And besides, they were supposed to be working on an album.

Frey and Henley did have some songs, and, as they worked through them, discovered that a theme was emerging. Frey said they had no concept album in mind. "But when we wrote 'Life in the Fast Lane' and started working on 'Hotel California' and 'New Kid In Town' with J.D., we knew we were heading down a long and twisted corridor and we just stayed with it. Songs from the dark side – the Eagles take a look at the seamy underbelly of L.A. – the flip side of fame and failure, love and money."

The title song was triggered by Don Felder, who came up with the guitar intro and gave Frey and Henley a demo tape. "It immediately got our attention," said Frey. "The first working title, the name we gave it, was 'Mexican Reggae'." (Frey recalled Henley dubbing it "Mexican Bolero" at first.) To Felder, who created the opening guitar riff on a twelve-string acoustic, the song encapsulated his life. "There was some Maundy Quintet bass, some basic Paul Hillis classical phrasing, some free-form Flow-style solos with a bit of Miles Davis thrown in, and some good old Elvis Presley rock 'n' roll guitar," he wrote in *Heaven and Hell*. "I could imagine the harmonies that would go with it would be very Crosby, Stills & Nash and sounded positively sun-kissed. It was, I later realized, the soundtrack of my life."

To Frey and Henley, it was the soundtrack of a movie, and they aimed for a cinematic song. "We wanted this song to open like an episode of *The Twilight Zone* – just one shot after another," said Frey. "This guy is driving across the desert. He's tired. He's smokin'. Comes up over a hill, sees some lights, pulls in. First thing he sees is a really strange guy at the front door, welcoming him: 'Come on in!' Walks in, and then it becomes Fellini-esque – strange women, effeminate men, shadowy corridors, disembodied voices, debauchery, illusion… Weirdness. So we thought, 'Let's really take some chances. Let's try to write in a way that we've never written before.' Steely Dan inspired us because of their lyrical bravery … so, for us, 'Hotel California' was about thinking and writing outside the box."

It was also about the Eagles themselves, as ever-evolving musicians and human beings. "We were getting an extensive education," said Henley, "in life, in love, in business. Beverly Hills was still a mythical place to us. In that sense, it became something of a symbol, and the 'Hotel' the locus of all that L.A. had come to mean for us. In a sentence, I'd sum it up as the end of innocence, round one."

"Life in the Fast Lane", the song that became a catchphrase, was inspired by a criminal. Or, as Frey told it: "The true story is: I was riding in a car with a drug dealer… We were driving out to an Eagles poker game… He moved over to the left lane and started driving 75-80 miles per hour. I said, 'Hey, man, slow down!' He goes, 'Hey, man, it's life in the fast lane!' And I thought, 'Oh, my God, what a title!' I didn't write it down. I didn't have to."

And, later, when he heard Joe Walsh's guitar riff at a rehearsal, he said, "That's 'Life in the Fast Lane'. So we started writing a song about the couple that had everything and did everything – and lost the meaning of everything. The lifestyles of the rich and miserable… I really like this record. Plus, it made a statement: Joe Walsh was officially in the band."

"Wasted Time" was the Eagles' version of a "Philly soul torch song", said Frey, a long time fan of TSOP ("The Sound of Philadelphia") and of songwriter-producers Thom Bell and the team of Kenny Gamble and Leon Huff. "It was definitely us loving Thom Bell," said Frey.

"New Kid in Town", which Henley credits Souther for starting, is about "the fleeting nature of fame, especially in the music business. We were already chronicling our own demise." Henley laughed. "We were basically saying, 'Look, we know we're red hot now, but we also know that somebody's going to come along and replace us – both in music and in love.'"

With "The Last Resort", the Eagles made their most pointed social and political statement yet. It was Henley's song, said Frey, who called it "Henley's Opus". As Frey told Cameron Crowe in 2003, for the booklet accompanying an Eagles box set: "One of the primary themes of the song was that we keep creating what we've been running away from – violence, chaos, destruction. We migrated to the East Coast, killed a bunch of Indians, and just completely screwed that place up. Then we just kept moving west: "Move those teepees, we got some train tracks coming through here. Get outta the way, boy!"

RIGHT: Meisner, Frey and Walsh making their guitars sing, on stage in the USA in 1976.

8

THE FAST LANE

Hotel California was released in December, 1976 and shot into the charts. So did the first single, "New Kid in Town," which leapt into the Billboard "Hot 100" at No. 48 in mid-December. It displaced Manfred Mann's "Blinded by the Light" at No. 1 for the week ending February 26, 1977 before being bumped by Barbra Streisand's "Evergreen". That same week, "Hotel California", the single, entered the chart at No. 72, on its own way to the top.

LEFT: Don Felder on stage in Holland, May 11, 1977, playing a Gibson Les Paul guitar.

BELOW: The band on stage in London: Frey, Henley, Felder, Meisner and Walsh.

BOTTOM Don Felder playing a twin-neck and Joe Walsh with a six-string.

125

About all that Frey and Henley had in common now were stomach ailments. It's unlikely that they shared their bottles of Mylanta.

They might have, back in those days and nights together on Briarcrest Lane. But, while they meshed as songwriters and men on the prowl, they began to jostle for the position of leader of the Eagles. Henley and Frey had a blowout, and the former moved out, and into Azoff's home. *The Odd Couple* were no more. Now, they were, simply, at odds.

And, on tour, any irritation could lead to a firing. That happened in Canada, where a hotel reservation for Henley was botched. He had long-time road manager Richie Fernandez fired, calling him a "pothead" that he could no longer depend on. The loss of the popular Fernandez upset the rest of the road crew, irrespective of their allegiance to Don, Glenn, or both. Paranoia set in, Berry said.

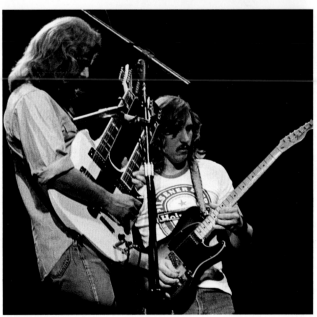

Elsewhere in the hotels the Eagles occupied, a crazed Walsh, sometimes abetted by manager Azoff, would try to destroy rooms and furnishings, often with the help of a chainsaw that Walsh carried on tour for that very purpose. In fact, the saw was a gift from Azoff's public relations assistant, Larry Solters.

But mornings brought reality. The tour, said Randy Meisner, became a serial, a soap opera. Frey and Henley continued to fight, and not just about the band's direction. They argued about hotel accommodations and finances, and even when they agreed, the results could be demoralizing, as when it was decided that the band would stay in better hotels than the crew. So much for family.

As the tour rolled on, it became clear that all decisions were being made by Azoff and the at-odds couple. It became almost as funny as the situation comedy after which Henley and Frey were named. The two principal Eagles weren't speaking to each other, so anyone – even fellow Eagles – who needed a question answered had to go through Frey's or Henley's chief roadies. When Frey and Henley wanted to talk, they did it through their respective roadies. It was a reality show before its time.

But it wasn't just the "Glenn and Don" show. They didn't limit their attacks to each other. Henley also disliked Walsh, not only for his showboating, but also because, he said, Walsh had tried to get his drummer, Joe Vitale, into the band as a member. Vitale had served as a second drummer for the Eagles, freeing Henley to step up front. But Henley, said Felder, saw Vitale as a threat.

Meantime, Frey had issues with Felder, while Henley did not. Frey and Henley also had problems with Meisner, who had been complaining about his diminished role as a songwriter

LEFT: Randy Meisner (left), in one of the last publicity phtographs he was to appear in before he left, 1977.

ABOVE: Frey, Meisner, Henley and Walsh rocking out on stage in Rotterdam, Holland, May 11, 1977.

in the band, and about the Eagles' devolution from music-based friendships to "all business". He was also unhappy with Henley's "star trip".

On stage, Meisner was still shy after all these years. He avoided the spotlight – literally. On his solos, he requested that his light be blue, not white. Even then, said Henley, he would move away from it. But on occasion, he'd have a fun moment with Walsh, joining him in a Chuck Berry duck-walk when they played "Carol". "That used to really burn Don's ass," said Randy, "and he'd let the both of us know. Joe would just laugh it off, but I couldn't."

One night, Walsh and Felder were complaining about Frey and Henley. "Hey, I feel kind of left out, too," Meisner responded. "Why don't we just start a little trio or something – our own group?" Meisner recalled Walsh and Felder nodding in agreement: "Yeah, yeah!" But, he added, the two had just returned from the Coconut Grove and "were kind of buzzed".

A few weeks later, the Eagles were in Knoxville, and Meisner was down with ulcers and the flu. He got through a concert, but when the encore call came, he didn't answer. "No way," he told his band mates. Frey confronted him. "You pussy!" he shouted. Meisner took a swing at him. After a brief scuffle, they were

separated, but, before leaving, Frey took a towel, wiped his face off, and threw it at Meisner.

Meisner seemed to be looking for a way out, and he found it. "When the tour ended, I left the band," said Meisner. "Those last days on the road were the worst. Nobody was talking to me, or would hang after the shows, or do anything. I was made an outcast from the band I'd helped start."

In June, "Life in the Fast Lane" had become the third hit off *Hotel California*, reaching No. 11 on *Billboard*. But Meisner chose life at the speed limit. As Don Felder put it, "He'd reached a point where his heart told him to stop."

To replace Meisner, the Eagles tapped Timothy B. Schmit, the musician who'd replaced him once before, in Poco. Like Meisner, Schmit was a solid bass player with a tenor voice that could soar to the rafters. With his boyish good looks (he was the same age as Henley, Felder, Walsh and Leadon), his gentle demeanor and his long hair, he was nicknamed "Woodstock".

But when it came to music, he was anything but laid back. Born in Oakland, California on October 30, 1947, he was the son of Danny Schmit, a traveling musician who played bass and violin. By age ten, the family was in

ABOVE: Meisner, Frey, Henley, Felder and Walsh on stage in Holland, 1977.

RIGHT: The new line-up: Glenn Frey, Don Felder, Don Henley, Joe Walsh, and new bassist Timothy B. Schmit.

Sacramento, where Timothy saw a teen rock band at a talent show. He had learned violin and could tap dance; now, he wanted to swing. He took up trombone, then ukulele, then bass guitar.

In high school, he listened to folk music by the Kingston Trio, Peter, Paul & Mary, and the Limeliters, and joined a local trio, Tim, Tom and Ron. Folk gave way to surf music and soon Schmit and his buddies were the Contenders, playing Beach Boys hits.

As with many teenaged American bands, Timothy's band next hopped onto the British bandwagon, becoming the New Breed. With Schmit, now 17, on lead vocals, they performed around northern California.

Schmit enrolled in college, studying psychology and gigging with his band, which, in 1968, became Glad. The band got a deal with ABC Records in Los Angeles and cut an album, *Feelin' Glad*. It was an overly optimistic title. The album flopped, but, while he was in Hollywood, Timothy met Richie Furay, co-founder of Poco. When Furay learned what instrument Schmit played, he invited him to audition for an opening in the band Meisner was leaving.

He passed the audition and had a nice seven-year run with Poco, surviving the departures of Furay and co-founder Jim Messina.

Schmit became the band's *de facto* spokesman as well as lead vocalist, and he also became an accomplished songwriter. But it seemed to be all for naught, as Poco never became a major force, despite their pioneering role in country-rock. Schmit soldiered on until one day, in September 1977, when he got a telephone call.

It was Glenn Frey, with a job offer. From the Eagles.

Deal.

Timothy B. Schmit had left a shaky band for what he thought must have been one of the most established and stable ensembles in popular music.

How wrong could one man be?

With his boyish good looks, his gentle demeanor and his long hair, he was nicknamed 'Woodstock'.

9

ENDGAME

It was as though the Eagles were made up to break up. Bernie Leadon once said that he knew he was on his way out when Don Felder joined, and that, in fact, he saw his Florida buddy as potentially helpful in easing the transition. Randy Meisner said that he had been thinking about leaving well before his final confrontations with Frey and Henley. "At the end of every tour, they broke up," said Irving Azoff. "The Eagles were breaking up from the day I met them…"

But here in 1977, they were, albeit with half of the original band gone, still the Eagles, still making hits, and still at war with the critics. In their view, they got no respect; no respect at all.

Here was *Hotel California* selling a million copies in its first week in the stores in December (It would ultimately sell more than 16 million). The first single, "New Kid in Town", a pretty and poignant song, was closing in on the No. 1 spot in February 1977. And now – only now – did *Rolling Stone* get around to critiquing the album. Even then, it was a measly three-paragraph, drive-by review, second-billed to a lengthy study by Dave Marsh of prog rock bands Genesis, Queen and Starcastle.

To the Eagles, this was an insult as well as being their second consecutive pan by the most important music magazine. Actually, it was a mixed review by Charley Walters, with a neutral opening – that the album showcased "both the best and worst tendencies of Los Angeles-situated rock" and that Henley, on five lead vocals, "expresses well the weary disgust of a victim (or observer) of the region's luxurious excess". The middle paragraph addressed the switch from Leadon to Walsh and the lessening of country and bluegrass influences on the band. Walters praised the title cut, along with "Life in the Fast Lane" and "Victim of Love". "Henley is superb on all three," he wrote.

If Henley was angry about the review (and he sure was), he probably was especially incensed by the concluding paragraph,

in which Walters criticized the "frequent orchestration" on the album, particularly on Henley's "Wasted Time", which Walters heard as "an over-arranged wash embodying the worst of rock-cum-Hollywood sensibilities". But the critic liked "the elegant fullness of 'The Last Resort' and its summarizing line: 'You call some place Paradise… kiss it goodbye'."

Screw elegance. Henley, who had taken to writing scathing letters to various editors, retaliated by giving an interview to one of *Rolling Stone*'s competitors, *Crawdaddy!* magazine. "Our songs just don't get enough attention," he complained, claiming that critics ignored his and Frey's work in favor of East Coast favorite Bruce Springsteen and their own buddy, Jackson Browne (who spent part of his youth in Greenwich Village and was friends with "The Boss"). "It's not that they don't look at us as good songwriters," he said, "but they just seem to emphasize the songs that were hits rather than the ones that weren't. They don't seem to think you can write a catchy tune that's a hit that means something… I think our songs have more to do with the streets than Bruce Springsteen's."

New York-area critics had not been friendly to the Eagles since their onstage remarks back in 1972 at Madison Square Garden, trumpeting their "song power" over punk rock. Five years later, the Eagles found themselves sharing airwaves and concert stages with new heroes like Springsteen and Elton John, hugely popular bands like Fleetwood Mac, Peter Frampton and Paul McCartney's Wings, corporate rockers such as Kansas and Supertramp, headline-grabbing punk acts like the Sex

LEFT: The Eagles were certainly not "out to sea" in 1978 — they had hit albums and singles and they played live all over the world to sold out crowds.

ABOVE: Glenn Frey taking a moment to relax with the whole band on a sailboat trip in 1978.

PREVIOUS PAGE: Don Henley sporting his now famous 'Bullshit' shirt for the *Rolling Stone* vs Eagles ballgame of 1978.

Pistols, safety-first pop artists like John Denver, Barry Manilow and Barbra Streisand, soul stars like Marvin Gaye and Stevie Wonder and myriad mirror-balled disco queens and kings.

The Eagles were right in there, and often on top of the pops. But they were always grousing about their treatment in the press.

"We felt like we'd been mistreated by the press from the beginning," said Henley. "*Rolling Stone* and some of the other publications and critics… All in all, we'd been abused by the press, so we developed a 'Fuck you!' attitude toward them, which pissed off guys like Jann Wenner all the more… We had this attitude that we didn't need the press, we could make it without them…so we just clammed up."

"We used to have a 'punch them on sight' list," Frey added.

The band's collective middle finger extended to the industry as a whole. When, at the start of 1978, they won several Grammy nominations for their work on *Hotel California*, Azoff refused to have the band perform on the television broadcast unless they were guaranteed winners. When the organizers refused to skirt their rigid rules for one artist, Azoff reportedly told the producers the Eagles would appear and perform. But they didn't turn up, leaving the producers scrambling to fill a huge void at the end of the ceremonies, just before the presentation of the biggest award for Record of the Year. The Eagles won that Grammy, one for the single, "Hotel California", and one for Best Arrangement for Voices ("New Kid in Town"). A flustered host, Andy Williams, had to accept the gramophones on the Eagles' behalf. They lost in the Album of the Year category to Fleetwood Mac's *Rumours*, while Best Pop Vocal for a group went to the Bee Gees for "How Deep Is Your Love".

I wrote about the Eagles snub for *Rolling Stone*. In that piece, Azoff said his band was in a Malibu studio, "tightening some tracks for the next album. That's the future; this is the past."

Actually, according to producer Bill Szymczyk, work on *The Long Run* didn't begin until March. Pierre Cossette, longtime producer of the Grammys (1978 was its twentieth anniversary

as a telecast), told me, "They were going to stay backstage in case they won. And if they didn't, they wouldn't be sitting out there." Azoff denied Cossette's assertion. "I never indicated, ever, that we'd be there," he said. Frey, of course, backed Azoff's story. "We had work to do, and the new record is more important than showing up and resting on past laurels," he told me. He had a problem with award shows, he said. "There's a credibility gap. Debby Boone wins Best New Artist, and Warren Zevon and Karla Bonoff aren't even nominated." Also, he said, "I don't want to be pushed around and herded back like I'm cattle, and pushed in front of some microphone and 700 photographers and stuff. It's not what I'm about." On the other hand, he said, the Eagles were happy to have won. "We were genuinely flattered."

Note that Frey spoke with me for the article, despite the Eagles' policy of not doing interviews. In fact, an outright friendly Frey sounded more like a reader than a hater. "Don and I were looking at the tenth anniversary issue," he said. "I thought it was an excellent issue. A lot of good stuff to read… *Rolling Stone* is the best, far and away, a cut above every other thing that calls itself a rock magazine."

This despite the magazine, which had moved from San Francisco to New York the previous year, having taken to sniping at the band, if only in jest. *Rolling Stone*, whose publisher and editor, Jann Wenner, was, like Azoff, not exactly basketball-player height, ridiculed the Eagles for losing some charity softball games. One exchange of insults led to another, and

LEFT: Irving Azoff, the manager of the Eagles, in 1978. Azoff has managed many other top acts in music.

RIGHT: Newest addition to the band, Timothy B. Schmit, relaxing on a sailboat by the sea in 1978.

BELOW: Joe Walsh playing guitar at the same concert, in NYC, October 1979.

RIGHT: The Eagles performing on *Don Kirshner's Rock Concert* TV show in 1979.

OVERLEAF: The band backstage in New York, 1979: Felder, Schmit, Walsh, Henley and Frey.

finally to the grudge softball game at the University of Southern California that opened this book.

When we spoke, we were three months from game time, and Frey was ready to play. He was hoping to promote it, get a big crowd out, and raise money for charity. (His wish came true; some 5,000 people attended, and the losing team donated $10,000 to UNICEF).

"We'll be down in Florida with all the pro teams, so we'll be picking up some pointers," he said. "We're close to submitting our roster. They want all the stars. I can understand if you don't want to play Hunter [S. Thompson]."

After their resounding victory, Frey and Henley teamed up to write an article for the magazine, headlined, "Eagles Land on RS" (as in "our ass," I assume). As they often did in their compositions, they scored. Their account of the run-up to the game and of the game itself was concise and witty.

Clearly relishing their chance to slam *Rolling Stone* in its own pages, Henley and Frey stated their case for hating critics. "It seems that we were all victims of some kind of petty cultural war between L.A. and New York. (You all must be aware that

rock 'n' roll is just an 'attitude'; singing and playing well don't really matter)." Some *Rolling Stone* critics liked the Eagles at first, they wrote, until they became successful. "After that, of course, it became totally impossible for any of them to accept us, because we all know that success is inherently evil…"

They reported a pre-game tiff between Azoff (a.k.a. "Industry Upstart") and Wenner ("Boy Publisher") over the Eagles wanting to wear steel-cleated shoes for the game. Wenner insisted on rubber cleats. "Someone might get hurt," he argued. "How exciting," Azoff replied. "Do your writers ever think about that?"

Frey and Henley, as scribes, also had fun with Joe Smith, the chairman of Elektra/Asylum and the man who was always pressuring them for product, describing the former Boston DJ as "former voice of the Boston Celtics… now part-time mediocre actor." This was because Smith appeared had in *FM*, a waste of celluloid about a rock radio station, produced by none other than… Irving Azoff.

Frey's love of sports came through in the article. After the playing of the national anthem – "Life in the Fast Lane",

of course – he and Henley recalled the Eagles' first at-bats: "Timothy B. Schmit, the Latino with the German last name and the samurai headband… drilled a line shot that nearly took off Eric Baron's glove at third base. This…was an omen. We would hit the ball hard all day long."

The Eagles scored three runs in their first inning and built a lead of 15-3 by the seventh. Wrote Frey and Henley: "Final score: 15-8. Peter 'Better tickets, better reviews' Herbst… looked dejected… His team had left 13 runners stranded while committing five errors. In the end it was errors that cost *RS* the game‍d. Their first error was to call the Eagles sissies in 'Random Notes'. Their second error was to compete with us in front of girls."

Good stuff. But, of course, the magazine gave itself equal space, and, while acknowledging that the Eagles were the better team, and nice guys to boot, made note of their penchant for misguided potshots at the press. Remember Henley getting upset about the magazine focusing only on the hits when, in fact, *Rolling Stone* had singled out "Victims of Love" and "The Last Resort" for praise?

After the game, Henley told one of the L.A. dailies about the critics he most despised, including the esteemed Greil Marcus, "who's too chicken to come out and play". Writer Mikal Gilmore quoted Dave Marsh's response: "He ought to take his foot out of his mouth. Greil wrote the most favorable review of *Hotel California* that ever appeared, so naturally he hates him. Maybe they'd like to try typewriters at twenty paces. You know, the Beatles didn't have to play cricket to justify *their* music."

But, after the game, at Dan Tana's next to the Troubadour, the band, the journalists and the celebrities bonded over drinks and Italian food. It wasn't any kind of a 'Third Encore' scene, but it was détente. For a while, at least.

The Eagles returned to Florida, to work on *The Long Run*. They also played some summer concert dates. The pressure just kept on coming. Elektra/Asylum wanted new product. The Eagles knew they were a lengthy run from any new album. "We weren't going to finish any time soon," said Frey, "so we cut a Christmas record in Miami. It was a fall day, by the way, and it was hot as hell. Perfect for a Christmas record."

9 Endgame

LEFT: Timothy B. Schmit on stage in 1979. The bass guitarist soon assumed vocal duties on a number of songs.

RIGHT: Glenn Frey playing live in 1979. In less than one year the band would have split, each member going separate ways.

They recorded a faithful version of Charles Brown's "Please Come Home for Christmas", which fit Henley's soulful voice just fine. And, for the flip side of a Christmas single, they came up with an ode to a hangover from a monster of a New Year's Eve, called "Funky New Year". The single reached No. 18, the first Christmas record to do so since the Chipmunks in 1958 and Brenda Lee's "Rockin' Around The Christmas Tree" in 1960.

Having satisfied their label for the moment, the Eagles faced the task of writing new tunes for that next album. They would ultimately come up with a mix of tried-and-true ballads and some pretty fiery rock-guitar work. It was a direct response to the music of the day, which sometimes sounded dominated by computers and disco balls.

That music, Henley said, almost drove him to "agree with the punk sentiment, even though I don't agree with their method, in the way that they play sometimes. But, rock 'n' roll does need a revival for damn sure! It's getting too slick and too weird and everything – it's all androgynous, heartless, gutless crap."

If, as they entered their thirties, the Eagles were beginning to sound like parents – well, they were maturing in spite of themselves.

As Henley put it to Anthony Fawcett and Henry Diltz in *California Rock, California Sound*, "We try to grow up a little bit between every album, get a new sense of values, because when we were young and starting out, it was easy to be an angry young man at everything. I mean, we were pissed off at the record business. We were out to get it. And then we got it. So we have to get a more mature set of values, I think. And deal with things that are more important… We're concerned with things now like nuclear power plants, whales and dolphins, cancer and heart disease and stuff like that, which you don't think about too much when you're a teenager."

The Eagles set a high bar with *Hotel California*. That album, said Frey, "will probably be harder to shake than *Desperado*, which we haven't shaken yet". He was talking in the midst of making *The Long Run*. Szymczyk's log shows that work, at his Bayshore Recording Studio in Coconut Grove, Florida, and

at One Step Up studios in West Hollywood, ran from March 1978 to September 1979. It was, by all testimony from various Eagles, torture.

This would be the Eagles' fifth album. That fact alone should have signaled to the band's two remaining original members what lay ahead. "The Eagles never expected to make more than two albums together because we found out we didn't get along," said Henley in 1975, after the release of *One of These Nights*. "But things kept getting better in spite of ourselves."

The first song the band tackled was "I Can't Tell You Why", and it came from the newest Eagle. "Timothy came in with the title and other bits and pieces," Henley recalled. "Glenn and I just wanted to surround it with everything we could. Glenn came up with that wonderful counterpart, very much a soul-record type thing: 'Try to keep your head, little girl'. With Frey playing the guitar solo behind Schmit's shades-of-Smokey delivery, the Eagles had one in the can.

Then, for a long time, came nothing. Walsh blamed *Hotel California*. That album's success left the Eagles "very paranoid", he said. "People started asking us, 'What are you going to do now?' and we didn't know. We ended up in Miami with the tapes running, but nobody knowing what was going on. We lost perspective. We just kinda sat around in a daze for… months."

Make that "years". "The romance had gone out of it for Glenn and me," said Henley, after completing the album. "*The Long Run* was not as good as *Hotel California* and it was an excruciatingly painful album to make. We were having fights all the time about the songs – enormous fights about one word – for days on end. It took three years and cost $800,000, and we burned out."

"The arguments and tensions," said Felder, weren't personal: "They were over the music and what should be done, and what lyrics should be put in, and what songs should be included, and who should sing them and who shouldn't."

Finally, in summer of 1979, over a year after first entering the studio, they broke through with "Heartache Tonight". "We knew then that we were off the hook a little," said Walsh. "We had a single." The song came out of a jam session involving Frey and his Detroit mentor, Bob Seger. "I think we were jamming on electric guitars," said Frey, "and then he blurted out the chorus." With help from Henley and J.D. Souther, the Eagles had a breakthrough song.

Next came "The Long Run", a title that Frey and Henley had had around for years. It was ironic, he knew. "Everything was pulling apart and we were writing about longevity. Well, even if we weren't living it, we were always able to idealize it in a song about the way we'd like to be perceived."

For Frey, the R&B fan, the song was also "about me just lovin' Tyrone Davis' record 'Turning Point'. We had done some slicker production like the Philly sound, but 'Long Run' was more like a tribute to Memphis with the slide guitars playing the parts of the horns."

With help from Walsh and Souther, Henley and Frey came up with "The Sad Café". With a title taken from Carson McCullers' novel, Ballad of the Sad Café, the Eagles sang a wistful ode to the days and nights of the Troubadour, which "seemed like a holy place, protected by amazing grace", where the emerging generation of confessional artists "would sing right out loud the things we could not say". But, said Frey, "The line that really resonates for me in that song is 'I don't know why fortune smiles on some and lets the rest go free.' There were so many of us aspiring musicians hanging around at the Troubadour."

The band moved from reminisce to a mix of oddball titles and sounds, including "Those Shoes", featuring Walsh and Felder on dueling talk box guitars; "The Disco Strangler", their way of saying "disco sucks"; "Teenage Jail", meant to draw parallels between high school and incarceration; and "The Greeks Don't Want No Freaks", with Jimmy Buffett, who had opened numerous Eagles concerts, joining in on background vocals. Frey tapped Joe Walsh's "In the City", which he'd cut for the soundtrack of the 1979 film, The Warriors, for the album. "I always liked the song and thought it could have been an

Eagles record, and so we decided to make it one," he said. With that, and with a song about a lecherous film producer ("King of Hollywood"), The Long Run was finally over. The band felt more relief than triumph.

The album was released in September 1979, almost three years after Hotel California. Although Henley deemed the record inferior, the public jumped at the chance to buy new Eagles music. "Heartache Tonight", "The Long Run" and "I Can't Tell You Why" all reached the Top Ten and enjoyed three-month residencies in the national Top 40.

Once again, critics both praised and panned the band. In the case of Rolling Stone, it was an all-out rave, written by senior editor Timothy White (who had not made it out to L.A. for the softball game) and given the lead spot in the record reviews section. White began by calling the album "a chilling and altogether brilliant evocation of Hollywood's nightly Witching Hour". He sang so many praises that you half-expected the Eagles to pop up behind him with a harmonic "oooh!"

Clearly gluttons for punishment (and, in the Eagles' case, its attendant rewards), and to support the album in the face of ever-increasing competition, the band set off on another tour and, inevitably, another round of backstage arguments and fights. Some of them were over benefits in which they'd agreed to perform. Early in 1980, they played at a fundraiser for California governor Jerry Brown, at the behest of Jackson Browne. Linda Ronstadt, who was dating the governor, and J.D. Souther also performed. But Henley was uneasy about the Eagles getting involved with politicians. "Politics is a dirty game," he said.

Six months later, Henley's views hadn't changed, but he went along with another political benefit, this time for Senator Alan Cranston. And this time, the dissenter was Don Felder, who said he didn't trust politicians. He liked Governor Brown, but didn't know Cranston and, at a press conference, made his lack of enthusiasm clear. Backstage at the Long Beach Arena, when Cranston's wife visited backstage, Felder responded to her greeting by saying, "Nice to meet you…" And then, as she walked away, he added a quiet "I guess."

Frey heard him and exploded. When it came time to hit the stage, Felder told Frey that his backstage tirade was unwarranted. "You're an asshole for doing that," he said.

RIGHT: Don Felder on stage, not long after the band released The Long Run, their last studio album for many years.

PREVIOUS PAGE: Don Henley playing shortly before the split in 1980.

RIGHT: Glenn Frey goes acoustic on stage in Oklahoma in 1980.

FAR RIGHT: Joe Walsh playing live in 1980.

On stage, in the midst of "Best of My Love", Frey walked over towards Felder and said, "Fuck you. I'm gonna kick your ass when we get off the stage." Felder said Frey continued to taunt him, counting down to their fight. "That's three more, pal," he would say. "Get ready." "No sweat," Felder replied.

After the encore, there was no fight. The rest of the Eagles scrambled into their individual limos and fled the scene. Felder took an acoustic guitar and smashed it against a concrete column, no doubt visualizing Frey as the column. He was shocked to turn and see the Cranstons standing nearby, looking shocked. Frey was also backstage. "Typical of you to break your cheapest fucking guitar," said Frey, after the Cranstons were out of earshot. Felder turned and left, heading for his limo.

The Cranston benefit – which came to be known as the "Wrong Beach" show – followed a string of concerts the Eagles had performed in Santa Monica, for a live album.

Back in February, the Eagles had won another Grammy, this time for "Heartache Tonight", for Best Rock Vocal Performance by Duo or Group. Since the Eagles had snubbed the ceremonies the year before, creating havoc, they were not even invited to the show. But the win reminded Joe Smith, the Warner Bros. chairman, that he needed some new Eagles product. As he'd told Irving Azoff before, he wanted a live album. He expected that worldwide sales of such an album could bring in as much as $50 million. The Eagles, he said, had been agreeable. Now, with all the tensions in the band, they weren't so sure. Still, they had four concerts in Southern California booked in July, and the record company was planning to record them.

As Smith recounted in his book, *On the Record*, he got a call one day just before the first of those shows. It was Azoff, saying the band was backing off.

"Irving says, 'The guys want to tell you themselves.' Glenn and Don get on the phone, and they say, 'Look, we really don't want to do this. We really don't want to spend that much time with each other. We could do a short tour and not record and be finished. But we promised you we'd do this, so we're going to give you a chance, if you can answer one question.'

I said, 'What's the question?'

They said, 'In 1971, the Baltimore Orioles had four 20-game winners. If you can name them, we'll do the album.'

God must have opened a recess in the back of my mind, and I named them: Dave McNally, Jim Palmer, Mike Cuellar, and Pat Dobson.

Glenn and Don said, 'OK, we'll do the album and we'll see you tomorrow.'"

During the tour and, especially, after "Wrong Beach", the Eagles were at dysfunction junction. When it came time for the guys to listen to the recordings and submit edits, or participate in re-recording parts and mixing the results, Frey refused to go to Miami, while the four others went, but on different days. Or they'd send edits by mail. Said Szymczyk: "We were fixing three-part harmonies courtesy of Federal Express."

Joe Smith, hoping for at least some new material to include as bonuses, offered the band $1 million a song for two songs. They refused, although, at one of their Santa Monica shows, they did perform "Seven Bridges Road", a Steve Young composition featuring pitch-perfect, four-part harmony, and Elektra/Asylum issued it as a single, reaching No. 21.

The live set was released early in November 1980. But by then, Glenn Frey had made a phone call to Don Henley to end things. Henley recounted the call in the August 1991 edition of GQ magazine, in an article entitled "The Second Life of Don Henley and written by Christopher Connelly: "It was a casual conversation that started out being about football. And then he interjected that he wanted to go do something on his own. He didn't necessarily mean that he wanted to break up the group, but it pissed me off so bad, because I always thought in my mind that, when the group broke up, we'd get in a room

PREVIOUS PAGE: Don Henley, here performing solo, enjoyed a successful post-Eagles career.

LEFT: Randy Meisner with Therese Heston, backup singer in his band the Silverados.

ABOVE: Glenn Frey opted for a radical change in fashion once out of the Eagles.

Common Threads

After Frey's breakup call, Henley remembered, he was scared. "For a few months I was pacing in the house and drinking a lot. That was really a rough time for me."

That was putting it mildly. Besides the end of the Eagles, there was a breakup with Lois Chiles, an actress he had been dating. While working on editing the Eagles' live album in Miami, he met and began dating another actress, Maren Jensen. Wanting to impress her, he suggested flying to his ranch in Colorado in a Lear jet one day in October. The pilot crash-landed the plane, burned out the brake pads, and the aircraft went through a cow pasture, where rocks tore off its bottom. In a panic, but thinking quickly, Henley opened an emergency door, threw Maren out and jumped out as the plane slowed down. "We almost got killed," he said. (Maren suffered only minor injuries.) When he received a $7,000 invoice for the flight, he turned it over to Azoff, who sent it back to the airplane company, sans remittance. On the bill, he wrote: "We do not pay for crash landings."

Henley went through an even more serious incident in late November. As he put it, "I did a stupid thing and got into trouble with the law." The "stupid thing" was having a party at his house and not knowing just who all the guests were. One of them was a 16 year-old girl who overdosed. Henley was charged with possession of various drugs and with contributing to the delinquency of a minor.

Henley said he did not know that she was under age and did not observe her taking drugs. He said the first respondents were from the fire department, who told Henley that, if he made sure she was all right, they would leave it at that. Paramedics arrived next, resulting in Henley's arrest. Henley later claimed that he was one of several victims of a police conspiracy against celebrities, particularly of the liberal stripe. "I was stupid and naïve, but it was obvious they wanted to hang me and put me away." He survived, "relatively unscathed", he said. He was fined $2,000, ordered to attend drug-counseling sessions and placed on probation for two years.

While Henley sorted things out, Frey began working on his first solo album, pulling in Jack Tempchin, his friend from the Longbranch Pennywhistle days (and composer of two of the Eagles' biggest hits) for inspiration. His solo debut, in May 1982, was entitled *No Fun Aloud* – for good reason, says Tempchin: "He was so relieved that he could just do anything he wanted. 'All right! Now I can kick loose!' It's a lot of pressure, having Henley with his perfectionism. On the other hand, that's what made it so great."

On his own, Frey reached No. 32 on the album charts, selling more than 500,000 copies and earning a gold record. It didn't approach the Eagles' recent sales figures. But could any individual band member do that?

Frey did well. He scored six hits in six years: "I Found Somebody" and "The One You Love" from his debut album; "Sexy Girl" from 1984's *The Allnighter*; "The Heat Is On", which he cut for the soundtrack of *Beverly Hills Cop*. It soared to No. 2 early in 1985. Also that year, he scored with "Smuggler's Blues" (No. 12) and "You Belong to the City" (No. 2), with boosts from a hot new detective television series, *Miami Vice*.

Michael Mann, creator and director of the series, had heard "Smuggler's Blues" from the debut album, on the radio, and didn't just put it in the show; he gave Frey a part. Frey then recorded "You Belong to the City" for another episode, and had a top ten hit. Meantime, his acting impressed enough that he landed work on two other series, *Wiseguys* and *Nash Bridges*, and in *Jerry Maguire*, a film written and directed by Cameron Crowe, who'd profiled the Eagles for *Rolling Stone* in 1975.

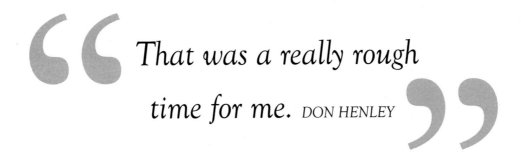

That was a really rough time for me. DON HENLEY

In 1988, "True Love" from his album, *Soul Searchin'* reached No 13. All together, Frey had compiled a six-pack of hits. But only one – "You Belong to the City" – made it into the Top Ten.

Meantime, Henley rebounded from his personal problems, tapped his immense songwriting and vocal skills and quickly proved himself capable of being the highest-flying Eagle of them all. He scored hits the way he used to score women at a 3E party.

Even before his first solo album, he hit the charts in a duet with Stevie Nicks, with whom he had what he called "a brief affair" in 1975. Their "Leather and Lace", issued in late 1981, hit No. 6. And when Henley went out on his own, in fall of 1982, he found a warm response. His album, *I Can't Stand Still*, included a nasty, angry attack on the media, "Dirty Laundry". No matter that he'd done his share of dirtying; his fans ate it up, and the song reached No. 3. Late in 1984, his second album, *Building the Perfect Beast*, produced a pair of hits, "The Boys of Summer" (No. 5) and "All She Wants to Do Is Dance" with Martha Davis of the Motels and Patty Smyth on backup vocals. The single peaked at No 9.

He had more modest successes with "Not Enough Love in the World" and "Sunset Grill", which reached the Top 40 in 1985. And when he produced his third album, *The End of the Innocence*, in 1989, he enjoyed watching the title track move up the Hot 100 in *Billboard* all the way to No. 8. Two other singles, "The Last Worthless Evening" and "The Heart of the Matter", got to No. 21.

The scoreboard for the decade showed Henley with nine Top 40 hits and Frey with seven. Joe Walsh had two. One was "All Night Long" from the soundtrack of *Urban Cowboy*, a 1980 film starring John Travolta and co-produced by Azoff.

Walsh also scored in 1981 with "A Life of Illusion," from his highly-acclaimed album, *There Goes the Neighborhood*. This was his first solo effort since 1978, when he issued *But Seriously, Folks…* while working with the Eagles. Walsh would maintain a rabid following, dating back to his days with the James Gang. Schmit and Felder, however, found themselves suddenly in a slower lane.

Schmit, who busied himself with back-up work for others, issued two solo albums, *Playin' it Cool* in 1984 (with support from Henley, Souther and Walsh) and, in 1987, *Timothy B*, which produced "Boys Night Out", which peaked at No. 25.

Felder, who composed and performed two tracks for the soundtrack of a 1981 animated movie, *Heavy Metal*, produced a solo album, *Airborne*, in 1983, with help from Schmit, Kenny Loggins, and Dave Mason, among others. It did not sell. It didn't really matter, he wrote in his memoirs. He was beginning to relax, to enjoy being home with his family. About the Eagles, he wrote, "The magnitude of what we'd become had torn us apart. It wasn't just Glenn. We'd all been ready to run from the machine."

The machine issued the official word in May 1982. The Eagles had disbanded. Azoff told Robert Hilburn of the *Los Angeles Times*: "In my opinion, they broke up because Glenn and Don realized they could both make great solo albums. They realized they didn't need the Eagles anymore. That's why you're not going to see them go out and do a farewell tour or a farewell album or a farewell anything. It's over. Period."

And, for the rest of the decade, the Eagles' lead voices were resolute that there would be no reunion, at least not until "Hell freezes over", as Henley said more than once. "There are some hard feelings," he said.

As much as Irving Azoff had preferred that the band could somehow keep working, he, too, wasn't holding out much hope. Years after the break-up, he spoke with Joe Smith, who'd left Warner Bros, for Smith's book of interviews with musicians and industry figures. "Some day they'll collaborate once again," Azoff said. "Many other bands have come back for reunion shot after reunion shot. They take the money and run. Glenn and Don don't do that. That should tell you something about their integrity."

Glenn Frey seconded that emotion. Soon after the official break-up announcement, he spoke about his newfound freedom, and about how excited he was to be his own boss and to make his own music. "That's why I know there'll never be an Eagles' *Greed and Lost Youth Reunion Tour*," he said.

With that in mind, Azoff knew that managing the Eagles now meant managing a catalog. (So did Warner Bros, which in December 1982 released a second volume of their greatest hits). In 1983, Azoff took an offer from MCA to run its record division for a salary of $500,000. "It's just time for a new challenge," he said.

RIGHT: Timothy B. Schmit performs for a solo album photo shoot.

For most of the Eagles – or former Eagles – life was just a challenge. In mid-1984, Frey's second album, *The Allnighter*, was rejected by Asylum. Joe Smith had left Warner Bros, and there was no longer a link from the executive level to Frey and his ex-band members. Each had received offers for solo albums; few had delivered, and, now, despite achieving gold with his first album, Frey was out. Fortunately, he could go to Azoff at MCA. He was quickly signed, and the album reached No. 22 on the charts, outperforming his first solo release.

Henley also switched record labels, agreeing to sign with David Geffen, who'd created a new label of his own called Geffen Records. It would be another big loss for Warner Bros as Henley's second solo, *Building the Perfect Beast*, turned out to be a monster in 1985. "The Boys of Summer" would win Henley a Grammy in early 1986 for Best Rock Performance.

With success came confidence, and, with the passage of time came willingness by Henley and Frey to meet, if not to jump into a recording studio together.

Snow began falling onto Hell late in 1984, when Henley saw Frey do a guest spot on David Letterman's *Late Night* show. He was promoting *The Allnighter* and watching, with pleasure, as his single, "The Heat Is On", was racing toward the top of the chart. Henley himself was promoting *Building the Perfect Beast*. He watched his former partner and felt a natural bond. The next day, he phoned Frey to say hi. Chitchat led to an agreement to meet on New Year's Day in Aspen, Colorado, where, 14 years before, they had become the Eagles over a month of practice gigs at the Gallery Club. Frey and Henley both had homes there. One day, they agreed, they might write together again. Ever the worrier, Henley told *Rolling Stone* about the possibility, adding: "There is a certain amount of worry that any music we might make together would be scrutinized unbearably hard."

Both Henley's and Frey's most recent solo projects were successes, and both were nominated for the then-new MTV video music awards, staged and broadcast out of New York City in September 1985. Henley's video for "Boys of Summer" won four shiny MTV moon-man statuettes, including the top prize of Video of the Year, while Frey won for "Smuggler's Blues" in the Best Concept Video category. Afterwards, the two, along with a few friends, met up at the Carlyle, where they worked through several bottles of Roederer Cristal Champagne – enough, anyway, that the subject of writing some songs together came up again. Frey remembered Henley saying, "We'll do it like the old days. We'll have a couple of beers, catch a buzz, and you'll go over to the piano and start playing some chords. Then we'll make up some cool lyrics and the next thing you know, we'll have ourselves a couple of good songs."

Frey said he missed working with his old partner, but that, even if they did get back together, it wouldn't mean an Eagles reunion. He pointed out that the band's management had received offers to play at the US Festival in 1982 and 1983. The fees had been $2 million and $2.5 million. Frey refused to even consider getting back together. "Any reunion of the Eagles would only serve to dilute what we've already achieved," he said in 1986, when he was 38. "I can't see myself at 41, up onstage with a beer belly singing 'Take it Easy'. Without a reunion, the Eagles are forever young, like James Dean."

Like Frey, Henley had mellowed over the years and welcomed his visits with Frey. "In some ways I think a lot of the conflict was imaginary," he said. "We were apart and the rumors would get back to us about something the other guy might have said and it might set us off. But every time we were actually in each other's presence everything was fine… there was no bitterness or animosity."

Their rapprochement kicked up, notch by little notch. In September 1989, Frey joined Henley on stage in Los Angeles, part of Henley's tour promoting *The End of the Innocence*. It had been five years in the making and a big success, staying on the album charts for 148 weeks and spawning three hit singles. But the reunion was brief, and in interviews they would continue to upset each other. Frey once said, to *Rolling Stone*'s Charles M. Young, "No one can suck the fun out of a room faster than Don Henley." Henley, for his part, would deride Frey's solo work as sub-par, or mock his appearing in commercials for a health club. And they'd stop talking.

Meantime, Irving Azoff resigned from MCA's music group and formed his own label, Giant, with a focus more on country than on rock music. His partner in the venture took him full circle: to Warner Bros. Country or rock, his main

PREVIOUS PAGE: Glenn Frey on a solo tour. This concert was in Minnesota in July 1985.

RIGHT: Joe Walsh attends the Orlando Vintage Guitar Show, February, 1993. The re-formed Eagles performed live a little more than one year later.

deal called for Henley and Frey to get a larger share of the pie than the three others. A grateful Walsh and Schmit had accepted the arrangement but Felder resisted. He had little recourse. The Eagles' manager was Azoff. His personal manager: Azoff.

Gritting his teeth, Felder fell into line and the Eagles began their *Hell* tour in late May, rolling through five of the scheduled six months until Frey was sidelined by a gastro-intestinal ailment that required surgery, forcing a 60-day hiatus.

Everything else happened on schedule: The MTV show; the CD; the DVD. The album reached No. 1, went multi-platinum and produced two singles, both new songs. The songs were "Get Over It" and "Love Will Keep Us Alive"; the other new ones were "New York Minute", "The Girl From Yesterday" and "Learn to Be Still".

To Felder's chagrin, the Eagles succeeded with "Love Will Keep Us Alive", a song he had demoed with the Malibu Men's Choir. The song, by Jim Capaldi (formerly of Traffic), Paul Carrack and Peter Vale, was one of eight that he had submitted to Azoff. The response, in a fax from his office, was a rejection. "The material you submitted wasn't strong enough," it read. And now it was a hit.

"Get Over It", a new Frey-Henley song, worked as a theme, of sorts, for the reunion – for the most part, the Eagles had gotten over the past. It was a response to tabloid television, said Frey. "I was so tired of professional victims everywhere you looked, all over the media. Don said, 'I have a title: "Get Over It".' I said, 'That's a song – let's write it!'… 'Get Over It' showed us that we could get together and write again. For that reason it's an important song to me."

Performing sold-out concerts wherever they played, the Eagles proved to be as big an attraction as ever. But things were forever changed. Walsh was sober; Schmit was making a good living again, and happy.

Felder was making a good living again, and discontented. He didn't like Henley and Frey commanding larger presidential suites at hotels and full-time staffs of assistants while he had a part-time guitar tech. He noticed how, in the credits on the DVD for "Hotel California", a song he'd conceived, he'd been bumped from first to third place in the credits behind Frey and Henley. "The Gods", as he called them, had escorts when they went down the hotel elevators to their limos, while Felder got his signal to leave from a security staffer over a walkie-talkie. "Sometimes," he admitted, "I let it eat me up too much inside." Taking a phrase from "Hotel California", he said, "It was truly a case of 'This could be heaven or this could be hell'.

11
THE EAGLES TODAY

Four years after Hell froze over for the Eagles and their fans, they were in Heaven: rock 'n' roll division. Well, it was as close to Heaven as the Waldorf in New York City could approximate. That was, as it often has been, the setting for the induction ceremonies for the Rock and Roll Hall of Fame.

In 1998, the Eagles joined seven other illustrious names, spanning early jazz and R&B to Sixties and Seventies rock, in the ritual of dinner, speeches and performances that precluded entry into the Hall of Fame. They shared the podium and the stage with Fleetwood Mac, the Mamas and the Papas, Santana, Lloyd Price, Allen Toussaint, and representatives for Gene Vincent and Jelly Roll Morton.

And when they were inducted with an affectionate introduction by their former opening act, Jimmy Buffett, they weren't just the Eagles who had reunited in 1994. They were all of the Eagles. Bygones were bygones, and Henley, first on stage, was trailed by Frey, Felder, Schmit, Leadon, Meisner and, in a hilarious suit with a brick-wall pattern, Walsh. Bernie and Randy were back.

They each took a turn at the podium. Henley covered all the bases, thanking his family, producer Bill Szymczyk (who attended the ceremony), Jackson Browne and J.D. Souther, and several estranged former associates, like Glyn Johns and David Geffen. "I want to thank Irving Azoff, without whom we wouldn't be here today."

Frey spoke up: "Well, we might still have been here, but we wouldn't have made as much money."

Henley laughed. "Right! As I've said before, he may be Satan, but he's *our* Satan!"

Henley also quibbled with the notion of a Hall of Fame. "I like to think of this award as acknowledging us not for being famous but for doing the work," he said.

According to Felder, the producers had told Schmit, Walsh and him to keep their remarks under a minute. Frey and Henley were exempted from this limitation. Schmit, no surprise, complied, saying brief thanks, including to Meisner, "for being there and paving the way for my being here tonight." Meisner, the only inductee to put on a tuxedo, was also concise, saying clearly sincere thanks to his family. Leadon had prepared a couple of jokes. "I'm really proud to have lived long enough to be indicted," he said. When Frey shouted, "Inducted!" Leadon pressed on: "I'd like to thank everybody on the grand jury who voted for me." He also expressed gratitude to some real forces behind his time with the Eagles, including Linda Ronstadt and John Boylan.

Walsh followed Meisner and drew the biggest hand of all of the Eagles, to the extent that Frey spread out his arms, as if to ask, "What's goin' *on* here?" He graciously thanked the Eagles' crew as well as Frey and Henley "for writing those songs; it makes my job real easy". And he acknowledged producer Bill Szymczyk "for finding me in the middle of nowhere."

Felder also thanked the Eagles' primary songwriting duo, as well as his wife Susan, "who put up with me for 26 years while we did this". Sadly, within a year, the marriage was all but over.

Frey was last. As he and Henley were wont to do, he found a negative vibe where there hadn't been one. "A lot has been made tonight about disharmony," he said. None of his fellow Eagles, current or former, had mentioned any such thing. But he made his point: "We got along fine," he said. "We just disagreed a lot. Tell me one worthwhile relationship that has not had peaks and valleys." The audience cheered. Frey, thus buffeted, went on to note that in all the years that the Eagles worked together, before and after their 14-year break, "the best of times rank in the 95 percentile, the worst of times rank in the very small percentile that obviously everybody but the seven of us have dwelled on for a long, long time. Get over it!"

With that clever song reference, the Eagles were inducted, and all seven members plugged in to perform "Take It Easy" and "Desperado". And then, as Felder recalled, they separated and disappeared into the night. All evening, he wrote in his memoirs, "The atmosphere was so tense you could have cut

PAGE 169: Don Henley on the *Hell Freezes Over* tour of 1995.

PAGES 170–171: All together for one night only — at the Eagles' induction to the Rock and Roll Hall of Fame in 1998: Randy Meisner, Timothy B. Schmit, Glenn Frey, Don Felder, Don Henley, Joe Walsh and Bernie Leadon.

ABOVE LEFT: Schmit on the *Hell Freezes Over* tour, 1995.

TOP: Henley, Schmit, Frey, Felder and Walsh in Minneapolis, 1995.

ABOVE: Don Henley's solo band perform in Holmdel, New Jersey.

ABOVE: Fans watch the band in Rotterdam, Holland in July 1996.

RIGHT: The 2001 line-up: Schmit, Henley, Frey and Walsh.

it with one of Joe's chainsaws." On stage at the Waldorf, he said, "everyone did a brilliant job of feigning back-slapping camaraderie, wearing forced smiles for the cameras." After the two songs, most of them hopped into separate limos. "It was just like the good old, bad old days," said Felder.

But it wasn't. Much had changed since their reunion tour, which had begun in May 1994, paused in October in deference to Frey's ailment, resumed in January and ended in May after grossing some $165 million. Add earnings from the *Hell Freezes Over* album, which hit No. 1 in its first week out and sold eight million copies, and two singles, "Get Over It" and "Love Will Keep Us Alive", and the Eagles were close to Azoff's $300 million promise.

The tour, Felder wrote, had no resemblance to the 3E days and nights of yore; there were strict edicts, issued from "The Gods", forbidding alcohol or drugs "so as not to tempt Joe. And there was to be no womanizing, because wives and children were now traveling with us."

Felder was the old-timer, having married in 1971. Schmit married in 1984. In 1994, Frey, was on his second marriage. He'd wed a Texas debutante in 1983, five years after they'd met. The marriage lasted five years. He then married Cindy Millican in 1988, and they had three children. So did Henley, who married Sharon Summerall in May 1995.

Although the Eagles were reunited, various members continued to issue solo albums, only to learn that audiences wanted Eagles, not individual birds. A 1995 Henley collection of his greatest hits, *Actual Miles*, didn't travel far. Nor did a 1997 release by Walsh, *Little Did He Know*.

But there were rewards to be found elsewhere. Early in 1996, the Eagles won three American Music Awards.

It was just like the good old, bad old days. DON FELDER

However, the Grammys blanked them, despite them earning three nominations for the album *Hell Freezes Over*, the single "Love Will Keep Us Alive" and the live performance of "Hotel California". (They would win two more Grammys, in 2008 and 2009, for songs from their 2007 album, *Long Road Out of Eden*). However, late in 1999, the RIAA named their *Greatest Hits (1971–1975)* as the Best Selling Album of the Century, with sales of 26 million units. The organization also added the Eagles to its list of "Artists of the Century" alongside the Beatles, Elvis Presley, Barbra Streisand and Elton John.

The Eagles, for all the honors, weren't quite done. Having added only a few new tracks to the *Hell Freezes Over* CD, they decided to try for one more album of original songs. They began talking about it in 1998, had several meetings – where, Felder said, he, Schmit and Walsh were told to submit CDs of any songs to Henley and Frey, who would decide what they liked. The two leaders would not have to submit anything to anyone, including a producer. They would produce themselves, and use studios built in Frey's home in Los Angeles and Henley's in Malibu. But it would be another

BELOW: Don Henley on stage during the Eagles concert at the Philips Arena, Atlanta.

RIGHT: The band played two nights in Atlanta, May 19 and 20. Joe Walsh on one of those nights.

FAR RIGHT: Glenn Frey in Atlanta. The 2003 tour ran from May until October that year.

long run. In fact, the recording would not materialize for nine years.

In 2000, Henley offered a clue that it would be a long time coming. "There's some disagreement about production values and song quality," he said. "There are things to be worked out before we can continue with that project." Not that Henley was idle. He produced another solo album, *Inside Job*, which reflected a man dealing with post-rock-star issues, including fatherhood. Supported by Frey, Randy Newman and Stevie Wonder, the album found favor on country radio and on formats like "adult-contemporary" and "light rock", and sold more than a million copies.

On the Eagles front, the new album was still in the distance. More certain bets were a live album or another compilation. Or, better yet, a boxed set of both. That's what the Eagles produced beginning in late 1999, when they agreed to perform on stage for the first time in three years They signed up for a short run of three appearances they called the Millennium Concerts. They began with two shows at the Mandalay Bay Event Center in Las Vegas, with Jackson Browne opening and Linda Ronstadt performing, and ushered in the year 2000 with a concert back

in Los Angeles, at the Staples Center, home of the Lakers basketball team and, often, of the Grammy awards ceremonies.

At intermission, audiences watched a short film produced by Frey, with images and music from the century just concluding. At midnight, they played "Auld Lang Syne". As an encore, they performed "Funky New Year", which was broadcast live on CNN.

The Eagles recorded the concerts to include as one of four discs making up *Eagles 1972-1999: Selected Works*, issued in late 2000. At those concerts signifying the end of a thousand years, Don Felder, who fought through a severe case of influenza to play, didn't know it but he was at the end of his own run with the Eagles.

Among all the Eagles not named Frey or Henley, he was the only one who questioned or refused the dictates coming from those two. What had started out an equal partnership had once again become the Glenn and Don Show. Felder rejected that status, as he objected to a new development when the Gods informed him, Schmit and Walsh that a new company, NEA, owned by Frey and Henley, would oversee *Selected Works*. They sent out an agreement for the others to sign. Schmit and Walsh

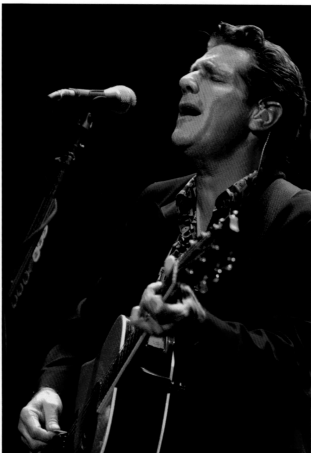

did so; Felder got into a shouting match with Azoff before finally relenting.

But Frey and Henley had had enough of Felder, and one night in February 2001, Azoff phoned him and said he'd been fired. The band's leaders, it was reported, felt that, beyond being a pest, Felder was overpaid. A shattered Felder first begged for reconsideration, then filed a lawsuit against Eagles Ltd, the band's corporation, for breach of contract and wrongful termination, among other charges. They reached a settlement in 2006. In the meantime, he was replaced on guitar by a hired hand, session guitarist Steuart Smith.

With Smith on board, the Eagles returned to the road in May, playing in Moscow, Finland, Italy and Ireland. They toured the United States and Canada in 2002 and then said that the end was near. In fact, it would happen in 2003 with a tour they glibly called *Farewell Tour I*. It began in May, in Richmond, Virginia. And, wouldn't you know it? It would, with an understandable break now and then, go on and on.

So did those plans for an album of all-new material. The album was still years away, but Frey and Henley did come up with some new songs. One of them came about in the worst

way. It was fall of 2001, and they were making another stab at starting the recording of the album.

"We loaded in on Monday, September 10," Frey recalled. "We were supposed to go to the studio on the morning of 9/11, but after hearing the news we called each other up and said, 'What's the point? I don't think there's anything worth showing up for today.' So we stayed home. And then that night Don started 'Hole in the World'."

Henley said he began with some chords and the phrase "hole in the world". Then he stalled for several months until the Iraq war began. As American casualties mounted, Henley found himself thinking: "One or two or three of our boys were – and still are – getting killed every day, which means somebody's daddy is not coming home. So that's another 'hole', a huge hole in somebody's life… There are holes in the information that the public is getting, both from the media and the government. There are holes in what passes for the logic of this administration's foreign policy."

With no new Eagles album in sight, "Hole in the World" would be heard in concerts and would serve as a bonus track for yet another greatest hits collection. This time, it'd be a mash-up of the two existing *Greatest Hits* CDs, and it'd be entitled *The Very Best of the Eagles*. For the millions who already had all the band's hits, the best feature was the booklet, featuring song-by-song insights from Frey and Henley, culled by journalist-turned-friend Cameron Crowe.

As always, Eagles songs ranged from the social and political – from "The Last Resort" to "Hole in the World" – to the deeply personal. Joe Walsh turned his battle with alcoholism into a sober, measured song, "One Day at a Time", which has resonated with audiences everywhere. He told me that the song took several years to piece together. "I just plain hit bottom, and it was a close call. There's life after all that. One thing that's giving me great satisfaction is a lot of people who're messed up, or dependent on something, are paying attention to it. And that's why I wrote that song. If I can just spread the word that there's life after that stuff, maybe I can help some people stay alive."

As it turned out, he had plentiful chances to spread the song. With guaranteed millions waiting on the road whenever they deigned to work, the Eagles continued their *Farewell I* tour in spring 2004 in Frey's home state, Michigan. They made their first tour of Asia in the fall, visiting Bangkok, Singapore, Hong

TOP: Schmit, Walsh and Frey on stage, November 14, 2004.

ABOVE: Songs from the "Farewell Tour I" were issued on DVD in 2005.

RIGHT: Don Henley performing on the same tour, this time in Sydney, Australia, November 2004.

11 | The Eagles Today

BELOW: Frey, Henley, Walsh and Schmit at a press conference for the "Farewell I" tour.

RIGHT: The touring continued into 2006. This live shot is from London, England's Twickenham rugby stadium in June of that year.

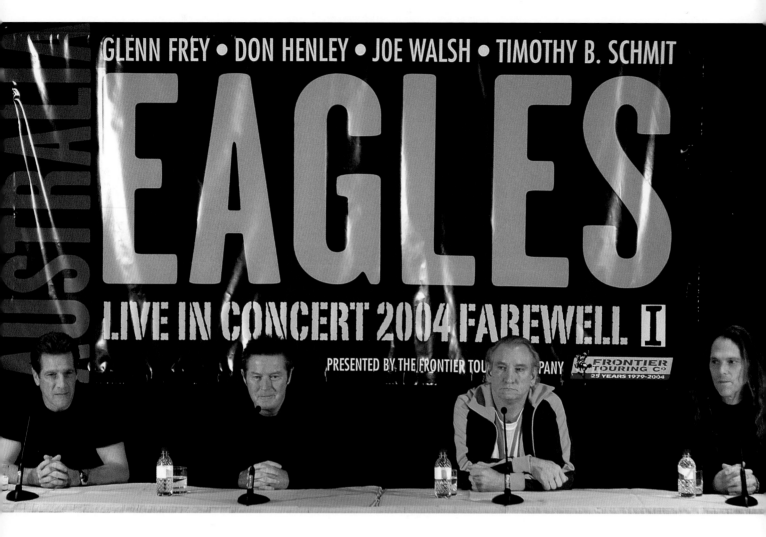

Kong and Japan. In November, they went to Australia to Perth, Melbourne and Sydney, where they had a rabid fan base, and where they videotaped concerts for a DVD, *Eagles Farewell I Tour: Live from Melbourne.*

The Eagles were unstoppable. In spring, 2005, the *Farewell* resumed, rolling from Charleston, South Carolina through 14 cities, with a week off halfway through, and winding down in New York City, which is where I caught up with them.

I saw for myself what critics had been saying in recent years. This band, who were once so insistent that they were rockers, were now in middle age and dressing like it. No more flannel shirts, worn jeans and boots. It was sport coats or dress shirts and slacks – at some concerts, dark suits that appeared to match, even. The only spontaneity and comic relief came from Walsh, who played with the audience, wearing a helmet-cam that put them onto the gigantic video screens while he cavorted and played guitar.

Their music: perfect. Backed by as many as nine extra musicians, they recreated their recordings note for note. And when I heard Frey introduce "Lyin' Eyes" by saying, "This goes out to my first wife: Plaintiff", it was clear that he'd said it more than a few times before. No matter. The audience lapped it up, along with his good-natured jab at the band still doing the *Farewell Tour I.* "It's a clever ploy by our management," he said. "He's plotting *Farewell VI* right now."

Backstage before the concert, I had asked Henley about a sixth farewell tour. "I don't think so. Not even a 'two', I don't think. We're supposed to do a few dates in September and October, and that may be the end of it. This *Farewell I* joke may actually be the truth."

LEFT: Don Henley on stage during day 1 of Stagecoach, California's Country Music Festival on May 2, 2008.

BELOW: November 2008 sees a smartly-dressed band performing on stage at the 42nd Annual CMA awards, Nashville, Tennessee.

RIGHT: Joe Walsh performs part of the Eagles' *Long Road Out of Eden* tour in Sacramento, California in April 2010.

OVERLEAF: June 7, 2009 and the band is still touring for *Long Road Out of Eden*, this time in Berlin, Germany's 02 World.

remarkable, nevertheless, when the Eagles performed at a televised music awards show for the first time at the Country Music Association's ceremonies in November 2007, playing "How Long".

A month later, they turned down an offer to be the half-time attraction at the Super Bowl with no explanation. The challenging but highly coveted spot went to Tom Petty and the Heartbreakers, led by the kid from Gainesville, Florida who'd learned some guitar from Don Felder, and whose early band, Mudcrutch, once included Tom Leadon, one of Bernie's younger brothers.

How could the Eagles pass up a chance to get global exposure before one of the largest audiences for any event on television? An opportunity to send millions of old and new fans rushing out to the nearest Wal-Mart? Perhaps the NFL didn't

offer them their usual $1 million-plus guarantee. Or maybe they thought their act, which usually began with four guys on stools strumming acoustic guitars and singing in harmony, might fall short of the 2007 spectacle staged by Prince. The Eagles were self-aware of their standing in music.

Joe Walsh, talking to Charles M. Young in *Rolling Stone* in 2008, thought back to the years leading to *Long Road Out of Eden*. "A whole new generation took over, and we asked ourselves, 'Should we change with the times?' We wrote accordingly and it didn't work because it wasn't us. We had grown-up responsibilities and shit I don't like very much. Very distracting, all this reality! So we came back to the idea that our only chance is to make an Eagles record like we know how, and it'll float or it won't, but we can't change with the times."

But, as it turned out, the times could change with them. Fans, unconcerned with music critics and musical pigeonholes, or with generation gaps, lapped up Eagles recordings and concerts, whether they were getting bargains at Wal-Mart or being held up, Doolin-Dalton style, for concert tickets priced in excess of $150. The Eagles were the soundtrack of their lives and they wanted to hear them, one more time.

Frey, Henley, Walsh and Schmit were hitting their sixtieth birthdays when *Long Road Out of Eden* came out. They celebrated by going off on a world tour to support the album, beginning at the O2 Arena in London. It ended in May in Utah and then, after a break, the band was back off to Europe.

The Eagles, who seemed, to those who knew them well, to be breaking up constantly, may never retire. As Henley told me, it's up to Frey. No matter. Eagles fans continue to hear their music on the radio and online, and, whether they're kids or original fans, they love it.

In an appreciation written for *Rolling Stone's* special edition on "The Immortals", Sheryl Crow spoke for many when she said: "Their melodies and harmonies have always been instantly familiar. 'Desperado', 'Take it to the Limit', 'Tequila Sunrise' and 'Best of My Love' are some of the best pop songs ever written. To this day, it simply doesn't get any better than that guitar riff from 'Life in the Fast Lane'."

To Crow's list, one can add "Peaceful Easy Feeling", "New Kid in Town", "Hotel California" (speaking of guitar riffs), "Lyin' Eyes" and so many others. Most fans don't know or care about the often-torturous process the musicians endured to create that music. They have no interest in the fights, the gossip, the tawdrier incidents and the dirty laundry. They appreciate the end results: music that continues to entertain, music that conjures a place and time, but is timeless.

The Eagles were often fractious, contentious, paranoid, egotistical, power-hungry, money-mad and ill-behaved. But in the end, little of that mattered. They did what they set out to do – and then some.

True, they were not the Beatles. (What band has been, or ever will be?) But the Eagles were smart enough to realize that fact early on, and to move on. By doing so, they became something similar to the forever Fab Four. They focused on the craft of songwriting, of building their writing on personal experiences, however painful they might be, as well as on a maturing social and political viewpoint. As Lennon and McCartney reflected the music they heard and loved as kids, so did the Eagles, folding in R&B, bluegrass and country sounds into their version of rock 'n' roll.

Like the Beatles, the Eagles grew with every album. Unlike the lads from Liverpool, Henley and company never were at ease with the media, never sought a high profile (witness their album covers, bereft of images of themselves) and never put forth an engaging personality or two to represent the band. Sure, they trashed hotel rooms and each other, but they didn't do it for the publicity.

Where they were most like their original role models was in their honesty. When it was over, one of them spoke up and they broke up. And when time healed enough wounds, and they realized that, in their absence, their popularity had maintained and they could profit from a reunion, they did the right thing – for themselves, at least.

Now, 40 years after first playing behind Linda Ronstadt and forming a band, they continue their run. Frey knows it can't last forever, but he wishes it could. In New York, he told me: "When you start seriously looking at the future and going, 'There's going to be a point where this is going to end,' I think it just makes all these moments more worthwhile and really gives us a chance to savor it. We're trying to spread this out and make it last a little bit longer."

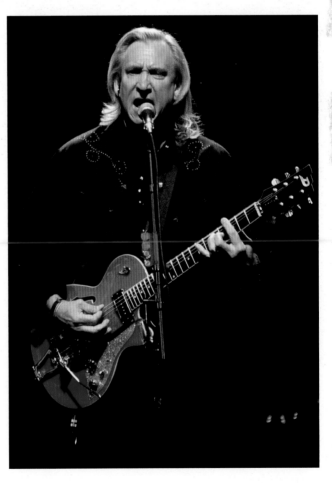

BIBLIOGRAPHY

BOOKS

Bowen, Jimmy and Jerome, Jim; *Rough Mix*, Simon & Schuster, New York 1997.

Einarson, John; *Desperados: The Roots of Country Rock*, Cooper Square Press, New York 2001.

Fawcett, Anthony and Diltz, Henry; *California Rock, California Sound*, Reed Books, Los Angeles 1978.

Felder, Don and Holden, Wendy; *Heaven and Hell*, John Wiley & Sons, Hoboken, N.J. 2008.

Fong-Torres, Ben; *Hickory Wind: The Life and Times of Gram Parsons*, St. Martin's Griffin, New York 1991.

Fong-Torres, Ben; *Not Fade Away*, Miller Freeman Books, San Francisco 1999.

Frame, Pete; *Rock Family Trees*, Quick Fox, New York/London/Tokyo 1980.

Hoskyns, Barney; *Hotel California*, John Wiley & Sons, Hoboken, N.J. 2006.

Jackson, Laura; *The Eagles: Flying High*, Portrait, London 2005.

Luerssen, John D., editor; *Eagles: Essential Interviews*, Rock Reader Books, Westfield, N.J. 2009.

Schipper, Henry; *Broken Record*, Birch Lane Press, New York 1992.

Selvin, Joel; *Ricky Nelson*, Contemporary Books, Chicago 1990.

Shapiro, Marc; *The Story of the Eagles: The Long Run*, Omnibus Press, London/New York/Paris 1995.

Singular, Stephen; *The Rise and Rise of David Geffen*, Birch Lane Press, Seacaucus, N.J. 1997.

Smith, Joe; *Off the Record*, Warner Books, New York 1988.

Swenson, John; *Headliners*, Tempo Books, New York 1981.

Vaughan, Andrew; *The Eagles: An American Band*, Sterling, New York/London 2010.

Whitburn, Joel; *The Billboard Book of Top 40 Albums*, Billboard Books, New York 1995.

Whitburn, Joel; *The Billboard Book of Top 40 Hits*, Billboard Books, New York 2000.

PICTURE CREDITS

" *We're the Eagles,*
from California. "

AUTHOR'S NOTE ON SOURCES

In researching the Eagles' story, besides the books listed in the bibliography, I consulted many other sources, including my own articles involving the band, from *Rolling Stone* to *TV Guide*. Other valuable material came from a wide range of media, including newspapers, liner notes, video interviews and various Eagles sites online.

Chief among the newspapers I consulted were the *Los Angeles Times* and the *L.A. Herald Examiner* for their coverage of the Eagles vs. *Rolling Stone* softball game, as well as for Robert Hilburn's interviews with the band, and the *New York Times*, and the work of Jon Pareles. The major magazine, of course, was *Rolling Stone*, where the Eagles were chronicled by such talents as Cameron Crowe, Anthony DeCurtis, Mikal Gilmore and Judith Sims, and Charles M. Young. (The reviewers of the Eagles' albums through the years are named in the text.)

Crowe interviewed Don Henley and Glenn Frey, focusing on songs and songwriting, for their collection, *The Very Best of the Eagles*. Another box set, *Selected Works 1972–1999*, features excellent notes by David Wild, Bill Szymczyk and Glenn Frey. Photographer Henry Diltz and Gary graphic designer Gary Burden's video, *Under the Covers*, from Triptych Pictures, captured the Eagles' album cover sessions for their first two recordings. (The video began as a CD-ROM, which I hosted.) Also helpful were *Hotel California*, a documentary by the BBC (British Broadcasting Corporation) and a collection of Eagles' appearances on television shows under the title *California Nights Interviews*, from Petal Productions. *Hell Freezes Over*, the Eagles' document of their reunion concert on MTV, from Geffen Records, was both entertaining and illuminating.

Bibliography